FROM
BEDER'S
KITCHEN

RECIPES AND REFLECTIONS TO RAISE AWARENESS
AROUND MENTAL HEALTH AND SUICIDE PREVENTION
FROM FOODIES ALL OVER THE WORLD

From Beder's Kitchen

©2020 Beder & Meze Publishing Ltd.
All rights reserved

First edition printed in 2020 in the UK

ISBN: 978-1-910863-71-8

Written by: Razzak Mirjan, Katie Fisher

Edited by: Phil Turner

Designed by: Paul Cocker

Photography by: Emma Guscott

Food styling: Liberty Fennell

Contributors: Michael Johnson, Tara Rose,
Paul Stimpson, Esme Taylor, Emma Toogood

Printed in Great Britain by Bell and Bain Ltd, Glasgow

Published by Meze Publishing Limited
Unit 1b, 2 Kelham Square
Kelham Riverside
Sheffield S3 8SD
Web: www.mezepublishing.co.uk
Telephone: 0114 275 7709
Email: info@mezepublishing.co.uk

CONTENTS

CHAPTER ONE - START YOUR DAY THE RIGHT WAY

CHAPTER TWO - HAPPY GUT, HAPPY LIFE

CHAPTER THREE - FAST FOOD (BUT NOT AS YOU KNOW IT)

CHAPTER FOUR - SOUL FOOD

CHAPTER FIVE - SWEET TREATS

FOREWORD
BY JOUDIE KALLA

When I first encountered my own struggles with mental health, I didn't know what to do, who to talk to or where to get help.

I couldn't find the words to describe the fogginess that followed me everywhere. My personality was robbed from me and I had to fake smile my way through things.

I found solace in the kitchen when I couldn't sleep or was riddled with anxiety and melancholy. I would go there to bake, cook and experiment to distract my mind from all things dark and dangerous.

Cooking gave me a purpose and, as time passed, things began to change. I decided that I needed to be honest with people about how I was feeling, which was daunting. However, the more people I told the more I realised I was not alone. This is not to say that I don't have bad days, but I have learnt how to manage them.

This cook book has and will continue to connect so many amazing people while creating a community of like-minded individuals. By making these recipes and reading the reflections of contributors' experiences with mental health in order to open up the conversation around these important issues, you are playing a part in looking after your own mental health. I hope that *From Beder's Kitchen* will allow you to get in touch with how you are feeling and to believe that you are able to speak about any emotion you may have.

As a community, let's be kind to others as we don't know what someone could be going through. Talk to anyone you feel safe with; you may also find that you have more in common with them than you realised. We are stronger together than alone.

In fact, I write this foreword in one of my lowest moments but I know I am not alone and there will be better days ahead. You just have to be gentle with yourself and nourish your body, not only with food but with who you surround yourself with, what you watch, what you listen to and most importantly the relationship you have with yourself.

I am proud to be an ambassador of Beder and to help this young charity as it honours the life of Beder Mirjan, with the hope that their work not only raises awareness but gives hope to those struggling.

We are all surrounded by people who love, want and need us to be here.

With love, Joudie

Cooking gave me a purpose and, as time passed, things began to change. I decided that I needed to be honest with people about how I was feeling, which was daunting. However, the more people I told the more I realised I was not alone.

ABOUT FROM BEDER'S KITCHEN

From Beder's Kitchen is a charity cook book bringing together amazing foodies all over the world while softly raising awareness around mental health and suicide prevention.

Our first cook book is, to some extent, a product of the coronavirus pandemic and the UK's lockdown. When Beder's in-person events were all cancelled, we had to move our work online by hosting events such as live cooking classes with a range of chefs on social media.

More than a hundred foodies responded when Beder reached out about the concept of *From Beder's Kitchen*, submitting a host of recipes and ideas with genuine enthusiasm and a desire to open up the conversation around mental health.

We chose 90 recipes to feature in the book, and many of these came with stories generously shared by their authors, from personal experiences to words of advice.

The key impetus behind *From Beder's Kitchen* is to softly raise awareness while encouraging everyone to understand that prioritising your mental health is not something to be apologetic or embarrassed about. Equally, if you are struggling with mental health issues or suicidal thoughts, it is important to know that you are not alone and it is certainly not something to be ashamed of. Opening up about what is on your mind can help you realise that plenty of people and resources are available to help you through difficult times.

For many people, cooking or baking is a form of therapy, and research supports the fact that cooking is good for your mental health; it provides an outlet for creative expression, a means for communication and can be an act of mindfulness. Of course, there are other ways to look after our mental health but creating delicious food at home for family, friends, loved ones or ourselves is a good place to start!

Each chapter has a different theme: Start Your Day The Right Way contains delicious recipes for breakfast and brunch; Happy Gut, Happy Life is filled with nutritious and healthy recipes; Fast Food (but not as you know it!) provides mouth-watering recipes which can be made in under 60 minutes; Soul Food is packed with everyone's favourite dishes; and Sweet Treats offers scrumptious desserts and baking recipes.

We hope you enjoy reading, learning and cooking with *From Beder's Kitchen* as much as we have enjoyed bringing this very special project together.

> The key impetus behind *From Beder's Kitchen* is to softly raise awareness while encouraging everyone to understand that prioritising your mental health is not something to be apologetic or embarrassed about.

ABOUT BEDER

Beder is a new charity raising awareness around mental health and suicide prevention through exciting events and initiatives.

We intend to increase understanding and reduce fear around the topics of mental health and suicide in order to overcome the stigma surrounding these incredibly important, yet underestimated, issues.

Our aim is to reach young, diverse and engaged audiences through a range of partnerships and provide educational, wellness and recreational activities designed to bring people together who share similar interests.

We hope that our soft approach to raising awareness around mental health and suicide prevention will help normalise the conversation around these issues. We want to help everyone learn about mental health as well as the work being done to support those in need, and to understand that you are not alone.

Beder was founded in memory of Beder Mirjan by his older brother, Razzak Mirjan, in November 2019.

As a family, we took the collective decision to start a charity in his name because we understand that it is not possible to rewrite history and have him with us today, but we believe that there are positives that can be found from our darkest days.

Beder has partnered with YoungMinds, a leading mental health charity, and Samaritans, an established and highly respected charity working across the UK and Ireland to reduce suicide rates. The aims of these partnerships are to harness the specialist knowledge of YoungMinds and Samaritans, as well as to promote and further both charities' incredible work.

Since founding Beder, we have organised a range of in-person events and initiatives that have included fitness, meditation and yoga classes in addition to football matches, mindful painting sessions and a music concert at Union Chapel in London. Following the outbreak of COVID-19 and the cancellation of in-person events due to the UK's lockdown, we transitioned to providing a range of online events such as live cookalongs and educational workshops. This has allowed Beder to reach people all over the world during the difficult times that we have all faced as a result of the pandemic.

There are many amazing people who help us achieve these goals and promote our purposes, not least our incredible ambassadors and supporters. These include Joudie Kalla, Marvin Sordell, Will Manning, Kieron Webb, Sarah Drai, Lawrence Price and Dr Joseph Spence, who have all joined our dedicated team of ambassadors to support Beder's work in their spheres of influence, which is greatly appreciated. If you would like to get involved with Beder, we would love to hear from you!

Whether you're interested in fundraising for Beder, representing the charity in a mass participation event, hosting your own event in support of us or simply having a chat, please do contact us for more information. To get in touch, email us at *inspire@beder.org.uk*.

BEDER MIRJAN

Beder Mirjan was a giant of a young man, with a witty sense of humour and an infectious laugh, who was gentle, caring, polite and kind natured.

He was incredibly intelligent, hard working and in love with anything related to aircraft, flying, computers and watches, among other things.

Beder was always surrounded by love and due to start university with a bright future ahead of him. However, he made the unexpected decision to take his own life at the age of 18 in April 2017.

We will never know the exact reasons for his decision, which makes coming to terms with his choice incredibly hard to process for those fortunate enough to have crossed paths with him, but we hope that Beder is now in peace and free from the dark thoughts that clouded his mind.

This is not how it was supposed to be, but, through Beder as a charity, we are working our hardest to normalise the conversation around mental health and suicide.

Our goal is to help people realise that it is okay not to be okay, and showing vulnerability or asking for help is not a sign of weakness. You are not alone, and those feelings that seem like something no one else will understand are feelings that so many others experience as well. Suicide is not inevitable; it is preventable.

It is important to never take those around us for granted and cherish even the simplest moments, as we never know what the future holds. It can be difficult to talk about someone who has taken their own life, or know what to say when someone brings their name up in conversation. That's understandable, but as we continue to mention their name or talk about the good times that we shared, we also give others the strength to share what's on their mind.

Our charity, Beder, and this cook book are in memory of Beder Mirjan.

It can be difficult to talk about someone who has taken their own life, or know what to say when someone brings their name up in conversation. That's understandable, but as we continue to mention their name or talk about the good times that we shared, we also give others the strength to share what's on their mind.

THANK YOU FROM BEDER

We are unbelievably grateful to everyone who has supported this project and helped play their part in bringing *From Beder's Kitchen* from a mere concept to a reality. Our list of thank yous is lengthy but incredibly important and, in no particular order, includes:

Each contributor who has supported this project by providing an amazing recipe, generously sharing reflections around their experiences with mental health and helping raise awareness around these important societal issues.

The Butti Foundation, with special thanks to **Hani Buttikhi**, and **Karen and Andrew Howes**, as without their unbelievable generosity and support this project would not have made it into a physical reality.

Our publishers, **Meze Publishing**, with special thanks to **Phil**, **Paul**, **Katie** and **Emma** for providing us with invaluable guidance from their years of experience and hard work to bring everything together in a short time frame.

Our incredible suppliers for their remarkable generosity including **Waitrose**, with special thanks to **Tor Alcock**, for supplying a wide range of ingredients; **Parson's Nose**, with special thanks to **Tony and Serena Hindhaugh**, for supplying the most delicious and flavoursome meat; **County Supplies**, with special thanks to **Robert and Elizabeth Hurren**, for providing the freshest and most beautiful fruit, vegetables and herbs; and **Jonathan Norris Fishmongers**, with special thanks to **John Norris**, for supplying a range of fresh, top quality fish and shellfish.

China & Co, with special thanks to **Nick and Liz Lees**; **Topham Street**, with special thanks to **Jo Harris**, and **Lisa Ommanney** for generously providing the most beautiful range of props, surfaces and ceramics which allowed us to bring the ingredients of every recipe to life for each photograph.

Morag Farquhar, as our prop stylist, for selecting the most beautiful props and creating beautiful colour schemes.

Emma Guscott, as our photographer, and **Liberty Fennell**, as our food stylist, for our beautiful front cover in addition to their creativity, support and hard work during very busy and demanding days on the photoshoot.

Megan Thomson, as our prop assistant, for making everything clear and accessible; our food styling assistants, namely **Rona Jones**, **Flossy McAslan**, **Kristine Jakobsson**, **Maisie Chandler**, **Lucy Hawthorne**, **Tessa Stable**, **Mandy Thompson**, **Deborah Rainford** and **Octavia Squire** for their energy, commitment and hard work, and **Georgina Cope**, **Liam Desbois** and **Becci Hutchings**, as our photography assistants, for their attention to detail and support.

Narroway Studio and **Kemble House Photography Studio** for your support and flexibility during our photoshoot at your beautiful studios.

Samphire Communications, with special thanks to **Zoe Wilmer** and **Rebecca Hopkins**, for their work in helping reach new audiences through a range of print and online media.

Planet Eat TV, with special thanks to **Tony Hindhaugh**, **Laura Connolly** and **Giorgia Young** for their enthusiasm, support and organisation to adapt this initiative into a series of episodes in a short time frame and allow us to reach an even wider audience.

Dulwich College, with special thanks to **Joe Spence** and **Fiona Angel**, for your love and magnificent support. The support that **Dulwich College** has provided to our family since losing Beder has been remarkable and we are incredibly grateful for everything that you did at the time and continue to do.

Joudie Kalla, for your continuous and invaluable support towards *From Beder's Kitchen* and, more widely, the charity as a whole; you are an amazing Beder ambassador.

Will Beckett of **Hawksmoor** for your incredible support and *"creating a bit of a problem"* for us which certainly helped to elevate the potential and reach of this project.

Zeina, for your continued love, support and encouragement since founding Beder and throughout this project which has been both time consuming and demanding.

Our trustees, partners and **supporters** for your invaluable support and belief in our new approach to raising awareness around these important issues.

We would also like to thank everyone who has bought a copy of this book, because in doing so you are playing your part in raising awareness around mental health and suicide prevention which contributes to our purpose as a charity, and as a family.

We are unbelievably grateful to everyone who has supported this project
and helped play their part in bringing *From Beder's Kitchen*
from a mere concept to a reality.

" NOW WE LIVE IN A WORLD OF CHOICE, INSPIRATION AND DELICIOUS DIVERSITY WHERE THE MORNING MEAL CAN BE ONE OF SHARED MEMORIES OF A HOLIDAY, A FLAVOUR, A LOVED ONE.

CHAPTER ONE

START YOUR DAY THE RIGHT WAY

It wasn't until the mid sixteenth century that a Tudor physician named Thomas Cogan said that it was essential to eat breakfast. Prior to him, it was debated that we shouldn't eat a morning meal at all! What a world!

From the evolution of pastries and croissants in Austria, the export of tea and coffee from China and Africa, and the more recent invention of convenience cereals, breakfast has and continues to evolve. Twenty years ago our weekends were less glamorous and far less social before the addition of brunch.

Now we live in a world of choice, inspiration and delicious diversity where the morning meal can be one of shared memories of a holiday, a flavour, a loved one.

The recipes in this chapter can kick-start a solo weekday before work, or set the table for a special occasion with friends, but they will all start your day the right way.

Michael Zee
(@symmetrybreakfast)

APRICOT & BITTER KERNEL JAM

PREPARATION TIME: 10 MINUTES, PLUS OVERNIGHT | COOKING TIME: 30-40 MINUTES | MAKES 1.75KG

We've used this simple but fabulous recipe for over 30 years in the restaurant, shop and bakery, only making it at the peak of the fruit's season. The fragrance of the simmering apricots lifts our spirits in the kitchen!

INGREDIENTS

1.25kg ripe apricots
800g granulated sugar
3 lemons, juiced

METHOD

Wash the apricots, cut them in half and remove the stones but retain them.

Place the apricots in a deep bowl, layering them with the sugar, then leave covered overnight to macerate. Meanwhile, crack the stones carefully and remove the bitter kernels from inside.

Blanch the kernels in boiling water for 2 minutes, rub away the skins and slice the kernels into slivers.

The following day, place the macerated apricots in a large stainless steel pan with the lemon juice and bring to a simmer over a gentle heat. Turn up the heat and boil gently, skimming occasionally, until the setting point is achieved.

The best way to check the setting point is by placing a saucer in the fridge while the jam is boiling. Every so often, drop a teaspoon of the jam onto the chilled saucer and return it to the fridge. After a few seconds, the jam should look slightly wrinkled as the saucer is tipped to one side. This will result in a semi-set jam, which I feel is best for summer fruit.

Meanwhile, preheat the oven to 180°c fan and lay six scrupulously clean jam jars on a baking sheet.

Sterilise them in the oven for 10 minutes. Boil the lids in a small pan of water for 5 minutes to sterilise them.

Stir the sliced kernels into the jam and fill the jars immediately, screwing the lids on firmly. Wait until the jam cools completely before labelling.

Focus on your goals and realise that while there may occasionally be obstacles along the way, stay resolute; aim for the vision in front of you. It also helps to talk. Find someone who you trust and admire. Talk ideas, thoughts, worries through with them. You may find that the older ones are the wiser ones.

SALLY CLARKE (@SALLYCLARKELTD)

EASY WHITE SOURDOUGH BREAD

PREPARATION TIME: I DAY | COOKING TIME: 50 MINUTES | MAKES I LOAF

There is so much love and attention behind a good sourdough. This is a tried and tested recipe and if you are new to sourdough or just a baking beginner, you can follow the same recipe using dry yeast.

INGREDIENTS

150g sourdough culture (nice and bubbly)

If you don't have a sourdough culture, use 2g dried yeast instead

270g warm water

400g strong white bread flour

10g sea salt

METHOD

In a bowl, mix the sourdough culture (or dried yeast) with the warm water until dissolved. Add the flour and mix well for 5 minutes, until no dry flour is left and you have a very shaggy dough.

At this point add the salt and knead the dough energetically on a work surface using the palms of your hands for 6 to 7 minutes. Once nice and elastic, shape the dough into a ball, using a scraper to help.

Transfer to a plastic container or bowl, cover and rest for I hour.

Grab the dough at one side, lift it up, and fold over. Repeat four or five times, moving clockwise around the bowl. Let the dough rest for 45 minutes, then repeat this folding process three more times, every 45 minutes. The dough will gradually become tighter.

45 minutes after the last fold, gently transfer the dough to your work surface without deflating it. Shape into a ball by slipping a floured scraper under the edge and then scraping it around the curve of the dough, like turning left when driving.

Do this a few times to build surface tension, cupping your palms around the dough and rotating it against the counter if needed.

Line a proofing basket or mixing bowl with clean kitchen towels. Dust these and the dough heavily with flour, then transfer it to the basket upside down, so the seams from shaping are on top. Cover the basket with a plastic bag and let the dough rise for 4 to 5 hours at room temperature, or until doubled in size.

Preheat the oven to 220°c and place a dutch oven or any other heavy-bottomed pot with a lid inside. Once the oven comes up to temperature, tip the loaf onto a piece of parchment paper. Quickly score the surface at a slight angle, almost parallel to the surface of the loaf; this creates the distinctive 'shelf' on top.

Place the loaf inside the heated dutch oven, put the lid on and bake in the preheated oven. After 25 minutes, take the lid off and bake at 190°c for a further 25 minutes or until the crust is golden and caramelised.

Cool on a wire rack for at least I or 2 hours. Enjoy!

I think the best way for people to try and see food is not just in terms of eating, but how it brings people together; look at meals like they are a moment of reunion with someone special, to connect and share stories, memories and feelings. When I was working at my first little restaurant in Australia, I used some traditional recipes from my home, Sardinia, and when cooking these I felt closer to home and created a community of other Italians living abroad. It was beautiful to be able to create a sense of home for them too.

FRANCESCO MATTANA (@OUR_COOKINGJOURNEY)

MORNING ELIXIR: JAMU JUICE

PREPARATION TIME: 10 MINUTES | COOKING TIME: 20 MINUTES | MAKES 10-15 SMALL CUPS

This gorgeous terracotta-coloured drink comes from Indonesia, where it is regularly consumed to maintain and boost the immune system. Once you have a healthy gut, you can start your journey to having a healthy mind.

INGREDIENTS

100g fresh tamarind seeds/pulp
350g fresh turmeric
500g fresh ginger
1 lemongrass stalk, smashed
2-4 tbsp honey
2 limes, juiced

METHOD

First, soak the tamarind in 400ml of hot water.

Put the turmeric and ginger (leave the skin on, but make sure they are clean) in a food processor with 500 to 600ml of water and blend to a thick liquid.

Add the ginger and turmeric liquid to a heavy-bottomed pot with another 750ml of water. Drain the soaked tamarind over the ginger and turmeric mixture, removing any pulp and pips, and stir.

Add the smashed lemongrass to the pot. Simmer gently for about 20 minutes. Don't let the mixture boil, as it will take away nutrients.

After the jamu juice has simmered, take the pan off the heat and stir in the honey and lime juice, then let the mixture cool down.

When it has cooled completely, sieve the liquid and discard the pulp and stringy parts of the ginger, leaving a smooth juice.

Place the juice in the fridge and drink a small amount (about 100 to 150ml) every day, stirring before each time you drink it because the goodness settles on the bottom. It should keep for up to 10 days in the fridge.

I discovered this amazing immune-boosting drink when I was extremely unwell with pneumonia and was trying to help my body to a full recovery with as little medication as possible. I was looking for something that tasted good and was cold, to soothe my throat, and when I learned about all the health benefits of this juice, I drank it every day for two weeks a month then made it again. It can cleanse your lymphatic system and kidneys, reduce inflammation in the gut, and help with digestion issues. It's also a fantastic antioxidant and can help with blood circulation and lowering cholesterol. This drink definitely helped me in so many ways, but be warned you will be left with a yellow-orange tongue!

If I was to give my younger self some advice, I would tell myself that I am stronger than I know, to trust my gut instincts and to say no when I don't feel comfortable with things. Also that with every bad dark day there will be sunshine coming after. Not everything stays the same and you just have to ride through it and sometimes not fight the anxiety and depression, but feel it, digest it and let it pass through you so you can heal what has damaged you.

JOUDIE KALLA (@PALESTINEONAPLATE)

MORNING CHAI

PREPARATION TIME: 5 MINUTES | COOKING TIME: 5-10 MINUTES | SERVES 1

Chai is synonymous with India. If you're Indian, it's usually the first thing you drink when you wake up and what you have after your afternoon siesta to give you that burst of life and energy.

INGREDIENTS

1 mug of any milk you like
1 English breakfast teabag
¼ - ½ tsp ground ginger or 1cm piece of fresh ginger, grated
¼ tsp ground cardamom (optional)
Pinch of black pepper
Pinch of ground cinnamon

METHOD

Here are two simple ways to make a morning chai at home:

The true Indian way is to boil all the ingredients together in a small saucepan for 5 to 10 minutes on a low to medium heat, then strain the chai into a mug and enjoy.

To make a quick chai directly in your mug, place the teabag in your mug as normal then add the quarter teaspoon of ground ginger, and a little sugar if you like.

Pour some boiling water from the kettle slowly into the mug, stirring as you pour, leaving enough space for milk.

Top up the chai with any milk you like (I use almond or oat milk) but again pour slowly and stir as you pour.

I created my chai spice mix with my mother and grandmother several years ago, which involved lots of trying and sipping and adding more of one spice and then a dash of another... we were all chai'd out!

Different parts of India make chai in very different ways, from boiling it with lots of grated ginger to simply crushing cardamom pods to using a masala spice mix, the way I do. However, the dominant spices are always ginger and cardamom, so you could start working with those to create your own favourite blend.

*Chai Excerpt and Recipe from Prajna: Ayurvedic Rituals for Happiness by Mira Manek

Stop worrying about what you can't change about the past or what you might be doing in a year's time, and just don't care what people say and think. It is so much easier said than done but if you try to say this out loud every day, you will start believing it.

MIRA MANEK (@MIRAMANEK)

COCONUT & VANILLA GRANOLA

PREPARATION TIME: 5 MINUTES | COOKING TIME: 10 MINUTES | SERVES 10

I always struggled to find a store-bought granola that wasn't loaded with unwanted ingredients like sugar or preservatives and still tasted delicious, so I created my own! I like to eat this sprinkled on Greek yoghurt for an after-dinner snack.

INGREDIENTS

250g rolled oats

30g almonds

30g pecan nuts

30g macadamia nuts

30g sunflower seeds

30g pumpkin seeds

25g coconut flakes

2 tbsp maple syrup or honey

2 tbsp coconut oil, melted

1 tsp vanilla extract

20g dried goji berries or cranberries (optional)

METHOD

Preheat the oven to 180°c fan while you chop the almonds, pecans and macadamias. Add all the ingredients except the berries to a large bowl and mix to combine so that all the dry ingredients are evenly coated with the syrup or honey and oil.

Pour the mixture onto two lined baking trays. Make sure the mixture is relatively flat but sticking together. It is really important not to overcrowd the granola otherwise the air can't circulate and it won't get crunchy.

Bake for 10 minutes in the preheated oven.

Set the granola aside to cool on the trays, then scatter over the goji berries or cranberries (if using) and transfer the granola to an airtight container.

TO SERVE

I like this with sliced apple and Greek yoghurt. Your granola should keep well in the airtight container, stored in a dark cupboard, for 2 to 3 weeks.

I believe that baking is therapeutic. I will get in the kitchen, put on some music and cook when I am feeling stressed or a little down. Food brings people together and the social element of sharing a home-cooked meal with friends and family can't be beaten. As a dietitian, I enjoy seeing my clients progress from only seeing the nutritional benefits of food, to the catalyst it can be for social connection and emotional wellbeing.

TALIA CECCHELE (@TCNUTRITION)

SMOOTHIE BOWLS

PREPARATION TIME: 10 MINUTES | SERVES 4

These bowls of berry goodness are protein-packed with chia seeds, milk and nuts
which help you kick-start your day and feel fuller for longer.

INGREDIENTS

2 tbsp chia seeds

100g natural or Greek yoghurt

300ml milk (rice, soy, oat, almond,
cow's milk or any of your choice)

200g frozen forest fruits or frozen
mixed berries

1 tbsp honey

75g mixed nuts (almonds, brazils,
cashews, hazelnuts or any of your
choice)

100g fresh blackberries

100g fresh blueberries

Bee pollen, for sprinkling (optional)

METHOD

First, soak the chia seeds in four tablespoons of water for 5 minutes to plump them up
or soak them overnight so they are ready to go when you wake up.

Measure out the yoghurt, milk and frozen fruits then put them into a blender with the
soaked chia seeds and honey. Put the lid on the blender and blitz everything together
for about a minute until really smooth.

Lay the nuts out on a chopping board and use a big knife to chop them into tiny pieces.

Spoon the blended fruit mixture into four bowls and decorate the top with the
chopped nuts and fresh berries, then sprinkle the smoothie bowls with bee pollen,
if you are using it.

*From Tilly's Kitchen Takeover

EMMA BARDWELL

BERRY KEFIR OVERNIGHT OATS

PREPARATION TIME: 10 MINUTES, PLUS OVERNIGHT | SERVES 1 GENEROUSLY

Water, dairy or plant-milk based, shop-bought or homemade, kefir comes in many forms.
Adding some to your breakfast means starting the day with a gut-loving dose of probiotics.

INGREDIENTS

60g frozen berries

3 tbsp kefir

3 tbsp plant-based milk, such as oat, almond or soya

2 tbsp Greek yoghurt

2 tbsp oats

1 tbsp chia seeds

1 tsp sweetener, such as maple syrup or honey

METHOD

Put all the ingredients into a bowl, stir well, cover and pop in the fridge for a few hours or ideally overnight.

When you're ready to eat, stir the overnight oats well and serve with more yoghurt, a mix of seeds and some fresh blueberries.

Tip: make a double batch and store in the fridge in an airtight container for up to 3 days.

There's something wonderfully therapeutic about cooking. I love sticking a podcast on, pouring a glass of wine and losing myself in creating something wholesome and nourishing; it's a great way to decompress after a stressful day. Good food doesn't have to be complicated or involve fancy, far-flung ingredients.
I made my brother, who died of cancer just before lockdown, a simple bowl of overnight oats every morning in the lead up to his death. It was one of the few meals he could face and brought comfort to both of us.
It's surprising in life how many of our most cherished memories revolve around food and eating.

EMMA BARDWELL (@EMMA.BARDWELL)

VEGAN BUTTERMILK PANCAKES

PREPARATION TIME: 15 MINUTES | COOKING TIME: 15-20 MINUTES | SERVES 2

These American-style treats are wonderfully fluffy, the perfect vegan pancakes for weekend brunches and so easy to make at home! Simply scale up the recipe to cook for more people.

INGREDIENTS

200ml soya milk

1 tbsp apple cider vinegar

2 tbsp plain vegan yoghurt

2 tbsp maple syrup

120g flour

1 tsp baking powder

1 tsp bicarbonate of soda

½ tsp ground cinnamon

¼ tsp vanilla powder or 2 tsp vanilla extract

Pinch of salt

Coconut oil, for greasing the pans

METHOD

In a jug, combine the milk and apple cider vinegar then set it aside for 10 minutes to curdle.

Whisk the vegan yoghurt and maple syrup into the curdled milk. Add the vanilla if using extract.

In a large bowl, combine your dry ingredients (flour, baking powder, bicarbonate of soda, cinnamon, vanilla powder and salt).

Pour the wet ingredients into the bowl and mix to combine.

Let the batter rest for a few minutes while you preheat two pans over a medium heat: one small 'egg pan' and one larger non-stick frying pan.

Grease both with the coconut oil.

Carefully drop spoonfuls of batter into the small pan until you have a layer about 1 or 2cm thick. Don't touch it and let it cook gently for about 4 to 5 minutes, or until the edges are starting to firm up.

Be very quick when you flip the pancake into the larger pan to finish cooking on the other side, and repeat this process until the batter is used up.

Looking after our mental health is very close to my heart, having experienced mental health problems in my family as well as going through anxiety and hormonal fluctuations that come with early menopause myself. To help with this, I set boundaries and acknowledge that I don't need to strive to be perfect, but instead accept my thoughts and emotions. If I could, I would advise my younger self to work on this acceptance instead of mentally marking things as 'something that's wrong with me'.

ROMY CALLWITZ (@ROMYLONDONUK)

STRAWBERRY CINNAMON TOAST

PREPARATION TIME: 10 MINUTES | COOKING TIME: 15 MINUTES | SERVES 2

The combination of strawberries and cinnamon, which I discovered through Niki Segnit's brilliant book The Flavour Thesaurus, is a surprising but delicious one. Perfect for a weekend brunch: less soggy than French toast, easier than pancakes!

INGREDIENTS

2 tbsp caster sugar

⅓ - ½ tsp ground cinnamon (depending how strong it is)

About 300g strawberries

About 1 tbsp flavourless oil

2 thick slices of good quality sliced bread (such as a white farmhouse batch loaf, you don't want anything too dense for this)

Soft butter

Half-fat creme fraiche, fromage frais or Greek yoghurt to serve

METHOD

Preheat the oven to 190°c fan.

Mix the sugar and cinnamon together. Hull the strawberries and cut each one in half.

Put the strawberries in a lightly greased baking tin and brush lightly with the oil.

Bake the strawberries for 5 minutes, sprinkle over one teaspoon of the cinnamon sugar and return to the oven for another 5 minutes or so, then remove from the oven. They should be warmed through rather than cooked and smell gorgeously strawberryish!

Meanwhile, toast the bread on both sides and spread one side generously with butter. Sprinkle the remaining cinnamon sugar over the buttered sides.

Put the slices on a baking tray under the grill and heat until the topping is bubbling.

Spoon the strawberries and their juices onto the hot cinnamon toast and top with a dollop of half-fat creme fraiche, fromage frais or Greek yoghurt.

I know how important mental health is and how its seriousness is not always recognised. Cooking has definitely helped me to look after my mental health. It's creative, repetitive, soothing and nurturing for yourself and others. I also try not to spend too much time watching and reading the news, stressing about things I can do nothing about, or worrying about what other people think of me.

FIONA BECKETT (@FOOD_WRITER)

IF I COULD GIVE MY YOUNGER SELF
SOME ADVICE, IT WOULD BE DON'T
BE SO HARD ON YOURSELF.

EVERYTHING COMES WITH TIME
AND PATIENCE; YOU DON'T HAVE TO
CHANGE THE WORLD RIGHT NOW!

LIBERTY MENDEZ
(@BAKINGTHELIBERTY)

LEFTOVER OKONOMIYAKI

PREPARATION TIME: 10 MINUTES | COOKING TIME: 30 MINUTES | SERVES 2-3 (MAKES ABOUT 6 SMALL PANCAKES)

Okonomiyaki is a pancake from Japan that literally translates as 'what you like, grilled'.
The first time I tried it was at a restaurant in Tokyo where the entire table is a cooking island.

INGREDIENTS

FOR THE PANCAKE BATTER

240g plain flour (00 flour if you have it)

1 tsp baking powder

180ml water or dashi

2 eggs

2 tbsp light soy sauce

1 tbsp vegetable or sesame oil, plus extra for frying

250g white or napa cabbage, finely shredded or grated

200g leftovers of your choice, chopped into julienne or small dice

TRADITIONAL TOPPINGS

Okonomi sauce (alternatively, use a combination of HP and Worcestershire)

Sweet Japanese mayonnaise

Aonori or slices of nori seaweed

Katsuobushi flakes

OPTIONAL TOPPINGS

Crispy onions or crushed crisps

Finely chopped spring onion

Sliced burger cheese singles

Crispy bacon

Fried egg

METHOD

In a large bowl, whisk the flour, baking powder, water or dashi, eggs, soy sauce and oil together until combined into a smooth batter. Stir in the shredded cabbage and your leftovers. You might want to prepare your toppings at this point too.

Add some oil to a frying pan over a medium-high heat. Add four to five tablespoons of the batter to the pan, and flatten it into a pancake about 10cm across.

Don't flip it until it has formed a crust on the bottom, which should take about 3 to 4 minutes. You may want to flip it back again to get extra crispy but remove from the pan when both sides are browned to your liking.

The traditional toppings are added in a specific order: first the okonomi sauce, a thin layer across the whole pancake, followed by a quick zigzag of mayo, then a generous sprinkling of aonori and lastly a few pinches of katsuobushi.

If you do this while the pancake is hot from the pan, the rising heat will make the katsuobushi move as if it's alive!

There are countless types of okonomiyaki within Japan such as Osaka, Tokyo and Hiroshima styles, all with distinct fillings and toppings. However, as you can imagine from the name of this recipe, it's really up to you what goes in it. Typically the okonomiyaki has a vegetable-heavy filling that's mostly shredded cabbage and carrot, with slices of bacon or sausage as the garnish. Now let's imagine you have the last of a stir fry, a few scraps of Sunday lunch, a random takeaway or something in the fridge that's on its last legs, looking a bit sad. Honestly, even if it's a single slice of pizza or a few falafel, chop them up and stick them in!

Dashi is the preferred liquid for the batter, an umami bomb made from seaweed, and is common now in many supermarkets. Water is also fine but remember to season your flour with a pinch of salt and pepper. The toppings are flexible, but at the least you should get yourself some aonori (a green seaweed powder), a bag of katsuobushi (paper thin pieces of dried tuna) and some sweet Japanese mayonnaise in a squeezy bottle. Alternatively, you can make your own sauce with a combination of regular mayonnaise and sriracha.

Eating has definitely helped me look after my mental health. Sometimes I find cooking incredibly laborious and boring, and I don't buy into this philosophy of 'meditative chopping'. Eating with friends and loved ones, though, and using food as a medium to exchange, rant and laugh is so important. Have as many shared experiences as possible; invite friends to everything.

MICHAEL ZEE (@SYMMETRYBREAKFAST)

JESSICA ROTHMAN

SUNSHINE EGGS

PREPARATION TIME: 5 MINUTES | COOKING TIME: 20 MINUTES | SERVES 2

This recipe takes inspiration from one of my favourite Turkish breakfast recipes, known as menemen. I've made a few edits to the traditional method, adding 'sunshine' with the saffron which instantly lifts my mood and transports me somewhere else.

INGREDIENTS

Pinch of saffron

2 medium-size tomatoes

1 white onion

1-2 tbsp olive oil

2 red peppers (I like to use the pointed type as they are much sweeter)

2 cloves of garlic

Pul biber (Aleppo chilli flakes) or chopped fresh chilli (optional)

2 tbsp tomato puree

Large pinch of salt

4 free-range eggs

METHOD

In a pestle and mortar, finely grind the pinch of saffron until it forms a powder.

Add a splash (a tablespoon or so) of boiling water and leave to brew while you prepare the other ingredients.

If you want to remove the tomato skins, use a sharp knife to just slightly cut through the skin of each tomato in a criss-cross pattern. Put the tomatoes in a bowl, pour over boiling water and leave for 5 minutes. Remove the tomatoes and, when cool enough to handle, peel the skins off.

To start the sauce, finely chop the onion while you heat a non-stick frying pan on a medium heat. Add a large glug of olive oil and begin to gently fry the onion.

While that begins to sweat and soften, finely dice the red peppers (roughly 1cm pieces). Add these to the pan and fry with the onions, stirring occasionally, for 10 minutes until both are very soft and cooked through.

Crush and peel the cloves of garlic then add them to the pan along with however much chilli you like, if you are using any. Cook and stir for just a couple of minutes. Roughly chop your tomatoes and add these to the pan alongside the tomato puree and stir to combine. Add two tablespoons of boiling water, the brewed saffron and salt.

Bring the mixture to a simmer and cook uncovered for 10 minutes, stirring occasionally until a thick sauce is created. If the pan appears dry at any point, add another dash of boiling water.

In a bowl, whisk the four eggs together using a fork. Pour this mixture into the pan and turn the heat down low. Stir the eggs into the tomato and pepper sauce, folding until they are just set and cooked (this will only take a couple of minutes).

Serve the eggs straight away. I like to finish these with a sprinkle of Aleppo pepper flakes and a generous blanket of fresh parsley (or other green herbs) alongside some warm flatbreads and salty feta.

You could even make them the centerpiece of an entire breakfast spread including fresh breads, chopped vegetables, preserves, cheeses, olives… enjoy!

When I'm in the kitchen, I can forget about the worries and anxieties of everyday life and instead immerse myself in what I'm creating. This feels like self-care, and the process is also very therapeutic for me. Other than cooking, I take time to slow down and focus on myself. This could be as simple as just leaving my phone on airplane mode for a few hours in order to fully enjoy reading a book, listening to a podcast, or something more active like taking a long walk in nature to find space and clarity.

JESSICA ROTHMAN (@SW3KITCHEN)

SWEET POTATO FRITTERS

PREPARATION TIME: 10 MINUTES | COOKING TIME: 10 MINUTES | MAKES 6

These are great served with smashed avocado and fried eggs for a healthy but tasty brunch. It's one of the meals I make when I am on a bit of a health kick but craving salty fried goodness!

INGREDIENTS

2 sweet potatoes, peeled and grated

1 dessert spoon of cornflour

Pinch of paprika

Salt and pepper

Fresh chives

1 small egg

Oil, for frying

METHOD

Squeeze the water out of the grated sweet potato then add it to a bowl with the cornflour, all the seasoning and chopped fresh chives to taste (saving a few for decoration).

Beat the egg then add it to the bowl and mix everything together.

Heat a non-stick pan with a good drizzle of oil and spoon in six even dollops of the mixture, shaping them into rounds.

Fry the fritters for around 5 minutes on each side, then serve them hot and stacked with smashed avocado and fried eggs, scattered with more fresh chives.

I love sharing recipes and having the ability to inspire others to get creative in the kitchen. Baking bread in particular has allowed me to get my hands stuck into something else (literally) other than the sometimes meaningless scrolling on my phone, and put a smile on other people's faces through my bakes.

LYDIA LEVY (@EATUPLONDON)

TRADITIONAL SCONES

PREPARATION TIME: 10-15 MINUTES | COOKING TIME: 10-15 MINUTES | MAKES 8

The secret of well risen scones is to get them in the oven as quickly as possible once the liquid has been added. The cheese and Marmite scones are my grandchildren's favourites!

INGREDIENTS

225g plain flour
2 tsp baking powder
½ tsp salt
60g butter
160ml milk, plus extra to glaze

FOR CINNAMON AND RAISIN SCONES

60g raisins
½ tsp ground cinnamon
30g caster sugar

FOR CHEESE AND MARMITE SCONES

60g strong cheese, grated
1 tsp Marmite

FOR DATE AND ORANGE SCONES

60g dates, chopped
30g caster sugar
1 orange, zested

METHOD

Sift the flour with the baking powder and salt into a large bowl.

Rub in the butter using your fingertips until the mixture resembles breadcrumbs.

Stir the flavourings for your chosen scones into the flour and butter mixture, then gradually add the milk as you bring the dough together. If you're using Marmite, stir the milk into it a little at a time, so the paste is evenly distributed.

Make sure all the liquid and dry ingredients have been well combined, then turn the dough out onto a floured board.

Knead very lightly and pat into shape, flattening the dough until about 2.5cm (1 inch) thick.

Cut out about eight scones, using all the dough, with a knife or cutter, then transfer them carefully to a baking tray. Brush the tops with milk.

Bake the scones in a preheated oven at 220°c for 10 to 15 minutes.

Allow them to cool then serve split and buttered.

My advice on looking after your mental health would be talk to people, be open, try to find a supportive environment and remember that just because others look happy and successful they may not be, and they may have similar concerns to you.

THANE PRINCE (@THANEEPRINCE)

BLUEBERRY BURST BAKED OAT SQUARES

PREPARATION TIME: 10 MINUTES | COOKING TIME: 25 MINUTES | MAKES 12

This super simple recipe is perfect for breakfast on the go or at home straight from the oven, and for those sweet tooth moments when you're feeling a little peckish but want something free from refined sugar!

INGREDIENTS

2 small bananas

175ml plant-based milk

2 tbsp nut butter

2 tbsp cacao or cocoa powder

220g gluten-free oats

100g fresh or frozen blueberries

METHOD

Preheat the oven to 200°c and line a baking tin with non-stick baking paper.

I like to use a 23cm square tin to get 12 pieces.

Mash the bananas then mix them with the milk and nut butter in a bowl.

Stir in the cacao or cocoa powder and oats until combined, then gently fold in the blueberries.

Tip the mixture into the prepared tin and flatten with the back of a metal spoon so it spreads out, reaching all the corners with an even thickness.

Place the tin into the preheated oven and bake for 25 minutes until firm to the touch on top.

Leave the blueberry oat bake to cool on a wire rack, then lift carefully out of the tin and cut into 12 squares. Enjoy! These will last for 2 to 3 days in an airtight container.

I had an eating disorder for nearly five years and have also struggled with anxiety. Baking and cooking were something I feared during my recovery, but once I started getting involved and being creative with my mum, I began to really enjoy it. Coming up with my own ideas and recipes gave me something to focus on, and cooking or baking for my family and friends made me realise that food brings us together and shouldn't be feared. It's so nice to finally nail a recipe and know that people enjoy it, and then you get to dig in too!

EMILY WHITE (@GFREE_EMILY)

NIAMH SHIELDS

BLACK RICE WITH COCONUT, BANANA & TOASTED ALMONDS

PREPARATION TIME: 5 MINUTES, PLUS OVERNIGHT SOAKING | COOKING TIME: 30 MINUTES | SERVES 1

This black rice feels like a real treat for breakfast. I usually have it at weekends when I have more time, but it is perfect at any time, and it is also a superb afternoon treat. Enjoy!

INGREDIENTS

FOR THE BLACK RICE
50g black sticky rice
150ml water
160ml tinned coconut cream
1 tsp honey (or to taste)

TO SERVE
1 banana, peeled and sliced (optional)
1 tbsp chopped toasted almonds

METHOD

First, soak the rice overnight and rinse thoroughly under the cold tap the next day. If you forget to soak it, rinse it a few times and you will be good to go.

Cover the rice with the water in a small pot with a lid, then cook gently over a medium heat with the lid on for 15 minutes, adding more water little by little if you need to.

When the rice has absorbed the water and is softening but still has bite, add two tablespoons of the coconut cream and honey to taste.

Put the lid back on the pot and set aside until ready to serve. Heat the remaining coconut cream over a medium heat and reduce it until it is nice and thick.

Serve the black rice warm (don't let it sit too long or it will get soggy) with the thickened coconut cream, sliced banana and toasted almonds on top.

If you haven't had black sticky rice before, have a look for it in the Thai section of Asian supermarkets. When cooked like this, it's a bit like rice pudding but deeper and richer. The coconut cream adds a feeling of decadence and it is perfect with most fruits so use what is in season, or just slice a banana on top as I've done here.

I like to add a sprinkle of chopped toasted nuts after the fruit for texture and flavour. My favourites are hazelnuts, pistachios and almonds. If I'm making this in autumn, I like to add some plums lightly stewed with a stick of cinnamon to serve on top of the rice. Stewed apple would be lovely too, and rhubarb in season is a joy, but the best thing to have on this rice is your favourite fruit, whatever that is, or even just add your favourite jam.

Cooking for me is an act of self-care. Cooking for one, as I do every day, is not something that I see as a chore, but time out from the daily stresses that I take to make something nourishing and delicious for me to eat. I believe that taking that time to nourish yourself should be a priority, even if it just takes 10 minutes. I know that is so hard to do when depressed, and I have been there, but start small, and make and eat simple things. Even a piece of fresh fruit can lift the spirit.

NIAMH SHIELDS (@EATLIKEAGIRL)

"I THOROUGHLY ENJOY FOODS HIGH IN FIBRE AND PRIORITISE VARIETY AS I GET BORED EASILY! I ALSO ENJOY FERMENTED FOODS LIKE KEFIR, SAUERKRAUT, KIMCHI AND KOMBUCHA.

CHAPTER TWO

HAPPY GUT, HAPPY LIFE

Looking back, good gut health has been inherent to my lifestyle since I was very young. However, it was just the norm and until relatively recently, I was ignorant to the importance of nourishing and caring for our gut. I'm still by no means an expert on the subject, but having studied for a nutrition qualification in 2016, I began to recognise its value. Growing research in the last decade has unearthed a community of trillions of bacteria living in our guts. This discovery has enabled us to better understand gut health as well as manage gut-related conditions, overall health and even conditions such as depression, diabetes and autoimmune diseases.

I consider myself very fortunate to have been raised on foods that have (hopefully) nourished my gut very well; I thoroughly enjoy foods high in fibre and prioritise variety as I get bored easily! I also enjoy fermented foods like kefir, sauerkraut, kimchi and kombucha; yoghurt appears daily on my menu, and I limit my intake of sweeteners.

In April 2020, my dad was diagnosed with terminal bowel cancer. It was not only a massive shock but a cruel reminder of just how fragile life is. By his own admission, Dad's diet has never been optimal in terms of cultivating a healthy gut microbiome which is even more impetus for me to prioritise my own gut health, learn more and hopefully inform and empower others to do the same.

Steph Blackwell
(@stephiblackwell)

STEFANI WEISS

GLUTEN-FREE SUPERFOOD BREAD

PREPARATION TIME: 10 MINUTES | COOKING TIME: 45-50 MINUTES | MAKES 1 LOAF

Cooking is like practicing mindfulness: it helps me be more present in the moment, and the process of creating each recipe is like therapy for me. Making this nut- and seed packed bread is good for your mind and body.

INGREDIENTS

90g walnuts

90g chia seeds

90g sunflower seeds

90g pumpkin seeds

90g sesame seeds

½ tsp baking powder

¼ tsp salt

4 eggs, beaten

100ml water

Coconut or olive oil

METHOD

Place the walnuts, chia seeds, sunflower seeds, pumpkin seeds and sesame seeds in a food processor or high-speed blender then blend them together until a flour forms.

Place the nut and seed flour in a big mixing bowl then add the baking powder and salt. For a savoury version, you could add chives, oregano, chilli flakes, pitted and sliced olives or any other flavours and ingredients you like at this stage.

Add the beaten eggs and the water, mixing well to combine all the ingredients and make a dough.

Preheat the oven to 180°c fan and grease a loaf tin with the coconut or olive oil.

Spoon the mixture into the tin, and press it down firmly using a spoon. Sprinkle the loaf with extra seeds if you like, then bake the bread in the preheated oven for 45 to 50 minutes, until the top starts to brown and a toothpick inserted into the centre comes out clean.

Remove the bread from the oven and let it cool completely while still in the tin.

Once cooled, cut the loaf into slices and enjoy them with your favourite toppings.

Having suffered from anxiety and depression, I'm always very passionate about encouraging conversations around mental health. Cooking has helped me so much with my anxiety. I also try to be more present and live in the moment, not in my head, to do something that I am passionate about every day, to walk in nature every day and to be more kind to myself.

STEFANI WEISS (@GLUTENFREE_STORIES)

CABBAGE KIMCHI

PREPARATION TIME: 10 HOURS | COOKING TIME: 30 MINUTES | MAKES APPROX. 2.25 LITRES)

Making kimchi is easier than you think and so much better for you than the mass produced ones. This kimchi is crispy, funky, spicy and sweet all in one bite. You won't be disappointed… and your gut will thank you!

INGREDIENTS

4 cups (950ml) warm water

1½ cups (165g) kosher salt or coarse sea salt

1 Korean cabbage or 2-3 heads of napa cabbage (between 1-1.5kg in total)

1 small onion, coarsely chopped

6 dried shiitake mushrooms

5 large dried anchovies (myulchi), head and guts removed

3 spring onions, coarsely chopped

32 cloves of garlic, 4 crushed and the rest left whole but peeled

1 x 12cm piece of dried kelp (dashima)

1¼ cups (125g) gochugaru (Korean chilli flakes)

7 tbsp fish sauce

5 tbsp salted shrimp (saewoo jeot), rinsed

2 tbsp sugar

1 x 9cm piece of fresh ginger, peeled and chopped

2 small carrots, julienned

6 spring onions, cut into 5cm pieces

105g Korean white radish (mu) or daikon, peeled and julienned

METHOD

In a large bowl, stir the warm water and half of the salt together until the salt has dissolved, then let it cool. Meanwhile, trim the bottom of the cabbage and discard any wilted or tough outer leaves. Rinse well, then partially cut the cabbage in half lengthwise, starting from the root end and cutting about halfway to the top. Using your hands, pull the cabbage apart to split them in half completely. Repeat so that each half is halved in the same way, which keeps the leaves intact and whole.

Loosen the leaves of each cabbage wedge so that they are easy to spread. Sprinkle the remaining salt over and between all the leaves, salting the core area more heavily. Put the salted cabbage into a large bowl cut-side up. Pour the cooled salted water over the cabbage, then pour enough cold water into the bowl to cover the cabbage, but don't overfill the bowl, as some liquid will be drawn out of the cabbage. Weigh down the cabbage with a plate so the wedges are completely immersed. Let this sit at room temperature for 6 to 8 hours, flipping the wedges over halfway through.

Rinse the cabbage wedges well under cold running water and gently squeeze out any excess moisture. Put them cut side down in a colander and leave to drain for at least 30 minutes.

Meanwhile, in a small saucepan combine the onion, mushrooms, anchovies, spring onions, four crushed garlic cloves and the kelp with two cups (475ml) of water. Bring to the boil over a high heat, then reduce the heat to maintain a simmer for 20 minutes. Strain the liquid, discarding the solids, and let the anchovy stock cool completely.

When the stock has cooled, use a food processor to combine the remaining garlic cloves, chilli flakes, fish sauce, salted shrimp, sugar, and ginger then process until smooth. Add enough of the stock to make a smooth paste, about one cup (240ml) in total. Discard any remaining stock. Transfer the spice paste to a large bowl and stir in the carrots, spring onions and radish.

Rub the spice paste all over the cabbage wedges and between each leaf. Pull the outermost leaf of each wedge tightly over the rest of the wedge, forming a tidy package. Pack the wedges into one or more glass (or other non-reactive) containers with a tight-fitting lid. Press a piece of plastic wrap directly on the surface of the kimchi, then cover.

The kimchi can be eaten at this young stage, or after it sits at room temperature and starts to get sour and 'bubble' (2 to 3 days). Store the kimchi in the refrigerator, where it will continue to ferment at a slower pace. I like to age mine for at least 2 weeks, but it really is down to your preference. Cut the kimchi before serving.

PLANT-BASED BUDDHA BOWL

PREPARATION TIME: 5 MINUTES | COOKING TIME: 5 MINUTES | SERVES 1

All my recipes are developed based on taste and what makes me feel good on the inside. When we let go of rules around food we realise that all the body really wants is balance, but everyone's version of this looks different.

INGREDIENTS

Olive oil

100g tempeh, sliced (or tofu)

60g asparagus, ends trimmed

60g broccoli, cut into florets

80g cooked black beans, drained and rinsed

80g cooked freekeh

½ an avocado

1 tbsp teriyaki sauce

METHOD

Heat some olive oil in a pan over a medium-high heat then add the tempeh or tofu.

Cook for a few minutes then add the greens.

Flip the tempeh to cook on all sides then add the black beans and freekeh to the pan for a few minutes to heat everything up.

Transfer the mixture into a bowl, top with the avocado and drizzle with the teriyaki sauce. Enjoy!

Food is so much more than fuel. It brings people together, it's enjoyable and helps to support us not only physically but mentally too. I had no interest in food until I understood how essential it is to our wellbeing. I only became confident in the kitchen around the age of 22, when I started to look at food differently. Cooking and baking is a form of self-care for me. I think there is something so powerful about spending time in the kitchen to cook yourself a meal and then taking time to really enjoy what you have made.
SOPHIE BERTRAND (@SOPHIESHEALTHYKITCHEN)

FERMENTED ASIAN SLAW

PREPARATION TIME: 7 DAYS | SERVES 4-6 AS A SIDE

This slaw started life at Pitt Cue Co. which is unfortunately now an ex-restaurant. But over the years some recipes have survived and evolved into what you see now. It's great with barbecued food or anything you like.

INGREDIENTS

1 white cabbage
1 large carrot
25g sea salt
50g ginger, peeled
50g garlic, peeled
50g white miso
50g organic honey
50ml soy sauce (white if possible)
2 limes, zested and juiced
250ml Kewpie mayonnaise
1 bunch of spring onions
½ a bunch of coriander leaves

METHOD

Shred the white cabbage and carrot, then sprinkle them with all the sea salt. Leave for 3 hours then press the salted vegetables, including the liquid that has been drawn out of them, into a fermenting jar.

Place weights on top to make sure they are submerged and if necessary, top up with bottled water.

Ferment for 2 days at room temperature then 5 days in the fridge.

When the fermented vegetables are ready, blend the ginger, garlic, miso, honey, soy sauce, lime zest and juice into a paste, then combine this with the mayonnaise.

To serve the slaw, remove some of the fermented vegetables from the fridge and squeeze dry. Mix with a little of the mayonnaise dressing and top with chopped spring onions and coriander.

I had PTSD for ten years before even being diagnosed; I think thirty years ago it had a different name, or maybe people just got on with it. It comes and goes, and can be triggered by the most ridiculous and unrelated things. But I've learnt that EVERYTHING passes, and everything is manageable if you just take a step back. Learn to let go of things you cannot control, avoid excess, and practice good sleep hygiene as this alone can save you. Oh, and you never know what someone else is going through, so maybe we should just give each other a break.

RICHARD H TURNER (@RICHARDHTURNER)

CALIFORNIA WALNUT & POMEGRANATE SUMMER SALAD

PREPARATION TIME: 5 MINUTES | SERVES 2

One of my favourite things to do with a salad is to include lots of different textures, not only to make eating them enjoyable but to provide a real diversity of ingredients too which is important for good gut health.

INGREDIENTS

4 large handfuls of watercress

2 handfuls of California walnuts

2 cooked beetroot, chopped

100g goat's cheese, torn into pieces

100g pomegranate seeds

1 orange, peeled and chopped

FOR THE DRESSING

2 tbsp extra-virgin olive oil

½ tbsp balsamic vinegar

2 tsp honey

Salt and freshly ground pepper, to taste

METHOD

Simply divide the salad ingredients between two plates, mix the ingredients for the dressing together and drizzle it over the top.

I absolutely love the crunch of the walnuts mixed with the creaminess of the cheese and the sweet punch of the pomegranates!

Cooking has helped me look after my mental health; it's a nice thing to focus on in the evening. I also prioritise a daily walk and sleep! Both the body and the mind need downtime to function optimally.

NICHOLA LUDLAM-RAINE (@NICSNUTRITION)

PRAWN & CHICKPEA HARISSA STEW

PREPARATION TIME: 10 MINUTES | COOKING TIME: 45-50 MINUTES | SERVES 4

This recipe was inspired by a trip to Marrakech that gave me so much creative flair, and when I returned home it was the first dish I made! Harissa originated in Tunisia but is common in Moroccan food too.

INGREDIENTS

2 red peppers, deseeded and cut into 2.5cm slices

1 tbsp butter

1 tsp harissa paste

2 tsp onion powder

1 tbsp smoked paprika

1 tsp ground cumin

½ tsp garlic powder (or 1 clove of garlic, crushed)

3 tbsp tomato puree

300g passata

1 tbsp olive oil

200g cooked chickpeas

150g fresh cherry tomatoes, halved

½ a lemon, juiced

1 x 324g pouch of Borough Broth Fish Broth (or stock)

Generous pinch of sea salt and black pepper

200g cooked king prawns

200g couscous

80g feta

Handful each of fresh parsley and dill (or other herbs of your choice, chervil and marjoram also work well)

METHOD

Preheat the oven to 220°c fan.

Place the slices of red pepper on a baking tray lined with parchment paper and roast for 25 minutes while you start the stew.

Melt the butter on a low heat in a large saucepan (with a lid) then add the harissa, onion powder, smoked paprika, cumin, garlic and tomato puree. Stir to make a paste.

Add the passata, olive oil, chickpeas, cherry tomatoes, roasted peppers, lemon juice, fish broth, sea salt and black pepper.

Bring to a low rolling boil. Turn down the heat and simmer with the lid on for 10 minutes. Add the prawns after 5 minutes, put the lid back on and remove the saucepan from the heat.

Leave the stew to rest while you prepare the couscous. This should take no more than 5 to 10 minutes to cook.

Divide the couscous between bowls, top with the prawn and chickpea stew, crumble over the feta and roughly tear the herbs to sprinkle them on top.

Finish with a final drizzle of olive oil and serve.

I would definitely count the kitchen as one of my happiest places and I find creating new dishes meditative in itself. Furthermore, I believe that feeding our body with nutritious and delicious food (the two are not mutually exclusive!) is vital for a healthy body AND mind. As a gut health specialist, it is also really empowering to know that the gut-brain connection is a powerful one that can be better supported by the food we eat.

EVE KALINIK (@EVEKALINIK)

ROASTED TROUT, SESAME MISO DRESSING, NORI PUREE & YUZU PICKLED DAIKON

PREPARATION TIME: 20 MINUTES | COOKING TIME: APPROX. 20 MINUTES | SERVES 4

This is a great dish for entertaining friends. You can prepare everything in advance and just cook the trout 'to order'. Pickles are naturally good for gut health as is miso paste, which has been fermented… plus it tastes delicious!

INGREDIENTS

4 x 180g skin-on pieces of boneless sea trout

4 handfuls of pea shoots

FOR THE YUZU PICKLED DAIKON

160g daikon, peeled and thinly sliced

4 tbsp yuzu juice

2 tbsp white wine vinegar

½ lemon, juiced

1 red chilli, sliced

1 clove of garlic, peeled and sliced

50g caster sugar

2 tbsp fine sea salt

½ tsp black peppercorns

FOR THE SESAME-MISO DRESSING

2 tbsp shiro miso paste

2 tbsp atari goma (or tahini)

2 tbsp honey

2 tbsp cold water

1 tsp pickled ginger puree

1 clove of garlic, finely grated

FOR THE NORI PUREE

8 nori sheets

100ml each of mirin, sake and soy sauce

50ml balsamic vinegar

METHOD

FOR THE YUZU PICKLED DAIKON

To make the pickling liquid, place everything except the daikon into a heavy-bottomed pan with 150ml of water. Bring to the boil. Place the sliced daikon into a bowl, pour the hot pickling liquid over the daikon then chill.

FOR THE SESAME-MISO DRESSING

Combine all the ingredients in a bowl and whisk well to combine. If you can't find atari goma, a sesame paste from Japan which comes in a white or black sesame version, just use tahini, which you can find anywhere. The results are similar but you may have to thin out the dressing with a little more water.

FOR THE NORI PUREE

Hold the nori sheets over the flame on your stove with a pair of tongs. Flip the nori over repeatedly until the sheet begins to dull in colour and crisp up. Be careful as it can burst into flames (but can be extinguished relatively easily when blown on).

Combine the mirin, sake, soy and balsamic in a saucepan and bring to the boil. Crumble in the toasted nori sheets and boil until most of the liquid has evaporated. Blend to a paste with a stick blender.

When you are ready to cook the fish, heat a little oil in a non-stick pan until sizzling. Meanwhile, use a sharp knife to make three or four score marks through the skin of each piece of fish. Season with salt and pepper then lay each fillet skin side down in the hot oil; it should sizzle immediately. Cook for 2 to 3 minutes until the skin is golden and crisp. Remove the pan from the heat and flip the fish over to the other side.

Leave it to sit off the heat in the warm pan for another 2 to 3 minutes.

TO SERVE

Smear a good dollop of nori puree over four plates.

Place a piece of cooked fish on top of the puree with some pickled daikon on the side (having drained off the liquid). Drizzle over the sesame-miso dressing, then garnish with the handful of pea shoots, or another delicate green leaf, to finish.

I have always taken a four-pronged approach to looking after my mental health. I look after my body, my spirit, my mind, and my community or family. I've found that if I focus on these four pillars, I keep myself well. Food nourishes the body and soul so I always try to create balance. Recognising interesting and healthy ingredients and learning to manipulate them in a considered fashion is what it's all about.
I think healthy food is often mistaken for being boring or tasteless, so throughout my career I have strived to ensure this is not the case.

MILES KIRBY (@FOODMILESKIRBY)

ROAST CAULIFLOWER WITH COCONUT & FERMENTED TURMERIC MEE REBUS

PREPARATION TIME: 15 MINUTES | COOKING TIME: APPROX. 1 HOUR | SERVES 2-4

This recipe is plant-based and gluten-free which, outside the professional kitchen, are the kind of dishes I eat regularly. Every now and then it's good to eat something indulgent, but look after your gut and body from day to day.

INGREDIENTS

1 cauliflower

Salt and pepper

Olive oil

20g fermented turmeric (alternatively, use the same quantity of fresh turmeric, grated)

20g galangal or ginger

2 cloves of garlic

2 red chillies

1 onion, peeled and diced

1 lemongrass stalk, chopped

2 lime leaves

120ml vegetable oil

1 large sweet potato, peeled and diced

4 ripe tomatoes, chopped

250ml coconut cream

100ml water or stock

20g miso

1 lime

METHOD

Trim the base of the cauliflower (I save the trim for making kimchi) and with a sharp knife cut an X into the core. Place the cauliflower in a cast iron pot with a little water in the base.

Season with salt and pepper, drizzle with a generous amount of olive oil then cook in the oven at 160°c fan until tender, which can take up to an hour or so depending on how large your cauliflower is.

Mee rebus is a southeast Asian noodle dish popular in Malaysia, Singapore and Indonesia. I've omitted the noodles, but the spicy potato-based gravy makes a delicious accompaniment to roasted cauliflower. To make the gravy, first put the turmeric, galangal or ginger, garlic, chillies, onion, lemongrass, lime leaves and vegetable oil in a blender. Blend to a smooth paste.

Heat a pan and add the spice paste. Cook for 3 minutes, stirring constantly, then add the sweet potato, chopped tomatoes, coconut cream, water or stock and miso.

Bring to the boil, then simmer for 10 to 15 minutes, or until the sweet potatoes are soft. Remove the pan from the heat and blend the mee rebus gravy until smooth.

Taste to check the seasoning, finish with a little lime juice and serve with the pot roasted cauliflower.

Mental health is something that I have been affected by for ten years. I've only recently started to talk about it, so to contribute to a project like this is amazing. Finding like-minded people has been a great help, along with sharing and talking. Eating well also plays a massive part in our wellbeing and it's important to look after our gut as it's all connected. The cleaner the food, the better we will feel, whether that's the very best organic aged beef or sustainably sourced fresh vegetables like I've used here.

DANIEL WATKINS (@CHEFDANIELWATKINS)

IT'S IMPORTANT NOT TO FEEL BURDENED
OR TO ASSUME THAT THE JOURNEY TOWARDS
WELLBEING SHOULD BE LONELY.

IDENTIFY A KEY INDIVIDUAL OR AN ORGANISATION
YOU TRUST TO SUPPORT YOU AT ALL TIMES,
AND BE AVAILABLE TO SUPPORT OTHERS WHEN
THEY ARE IN NEED.

ZAHRA ABDALLA
(@COOKINGWITHZAHRA)

GREG EMMERSON

BROCCOLI HEART WITH SABAYON & ANCHOVY CRUMB

PREPARATION TIME: 10-15 MINUTES | COOKING TIME: 40-45 MINUTES | SERVES 2

I once attended an event that's stuck with me ever since, where a chef from the States was highlighting food waste, in particular the parts of ingredients we might throw away. That creativity inspired me to develop this dish.

INGREDIENTS

FOR THE BROCCOLI HEART

1 large head of broccoli

4 tbsp Spanish olive oil

Pinch of sea salt

FOR THE ANCHOVY CRUMB

3 Ortiz fresh anchovies

150g breadcrumbs

FOR THE SABAYON

3 duck egg yolks

4 tbsp white wine (such as Chenin Blanc)

Squeeze of fresh lemon juice

METHOD

FOR THE BROCCOLI HEART

Remove the outer florets from the head of broccoli down to the stalk at the centre. Keep the florets for another recipe. Peel the thick outer layer from the broccoli core, then halve it lengthways so you have two long 'heart' pieces.

Bring a saucepan of water to the boil, add the broccoli heart and blanch for 30 seconds, then remove with a spoon and refresh in ice cold water. Repeat this process once more, then pat dry with a paper towel, brush with the olive oil and season with the sea salt.

Place the broccoli heart cut-side down on a baking tray and place in a preheated oven at 180°c fan for 20 to 25 minutes until a nice char has developed.

Once this is achieved, remove it from the oven and keep warm.

FOR THE ANCHOVY CRUMB

Place the anchovies on a baking tray lined with baking parchment in the oven at 70°c fan for 20 minutes, or until they have dried out. Once dry, remove them from the oven and transfer to a food processor. Add the breadcrumbs and blitz for 30 seconds to combine, then set aside.

FOR THE SABAYON

Whisk the egg yolks in a bowl over a bain-marie. Once they start to foam, slowly drizzle the wine into the bowl while whisking constantly. Keep whisking until the sauce thickens to a custard consistency and then add the lemon juice to taste.

TO SERVE

Spoon some of the sabayon into the centre of two dishes, then top with the charred broccoli hearts and a generous sprinkle of the anchovy crumb.

I've always found solace in cooking when I've been at a low ebb. It stimulates my mind and thought processes as it taps into your creative side, and I find it rewarding. When my mother passed away I was really struggling, I didn't cook for weeks, but eventually it helped me put structure back into my life. It was my mother who taught me to cook, so that would have made her happy to know it helped me. Communication is so important too, and whatever you do, don't think you have failed by seeking help from others.

GREG EMMERSON (@GREGEMMERSON_)

VEGETARIAN STUFFED PEPPERS

PREPARATION TIME: 25 MINUTES | COOKING TIME: 50-55 MINUTES | SERVES 4-5

Arabs in general and especially Palestinians love to stuff almost any seasonal vegetables for the best flavour. Growing up, dishes like this were made on the weekend, but were also festive enough for the holidays or when guests are expected.

INGREDIENTS

4-5 medium sweet bell peppers

3 tbsp extra-virgin olive oil

Salt and pepper, to taste

400g cooked short grain rice

240g cooked chickpeas, rinsed and drained

150g halloumi or feta cheese, diced

60g Italian parsley, finely chopped

60g fresh mint leaves, chopped

3 spring onions, chopped

2 vine tomatoes, diced

1 jalapeño, diced (optional)

1 tsp allspice

1 tsp sumac

½ tsp Aleppo pepper

¼ tsp ground cinnamon

¼ tsp freshly grated nutmeg

700ml tomato or marinara sauce

METHOD

Preheat the oven to 210°c fan.

Prepare the peppers by halving them lengthways then removing the 'ribs' and seeds to create a nice pocket for holding the filling.

Drizzle one tablespoon of olive oil over the peppers and sprinkle with salt. Roast in an ovenproof dish for 20 minutes in the preheated oven until the peppers are a little tender and caramelised.

In the meantime, prepare the filling. Put all the remaining ingredients except the tomato sauce in a large bowl and toss together to combine. Taste the mixture and adjust your seasoning.

When they have roasted, let the peppers cool enough to be handled, then divide the filling between them. Lower the oven temperature to 180°c.

Pour the tomato sauce into the ovenproof dish, then arrange the stuffed peppers on top. Bake for 30 to 35 minutes until the sauce is bubbling and the filling is piping hot.

Serve the stuffed peppers with a dollop of plain yoghurt and a green salad.

If you have extra filling, experiment with stuffing other vegetables such as tomatoes, courgettes or small aubergines. This filling is also delicious on its own. The peppers can be stuffed, covered and refrigerated up to 1 day in advance. Leftovers can be saved and refrigerated for 2 to 3 days.

Cooking is an act of patience and mindfulness as it requires close attention. It is an outlet for creative expression, a means of communication, and a rewarding way to express self-love and love for others. When you cook for yourself and others, it is an experience that creates a sense of community and wellbeing as well as heightening the love and joy of giving.

MAI KAKISH (@ALMONDANDFIG)

LENTIL & BULGUR PILAF

PREPARATION TIME: 15 MINUTES | COOKING TIME: APPROX. 1 HOUR | SERVES 4

Lentil and bulgur pilaf (mjadara hamra) is a very authentic recipe that is popular in the south of Lebanon and the mountains. I feel it is a very nostalgic recipe, reminding me of home.

INGREDIENTS

1½ cups (approx. 192g) green or brown lentils

¾ cup (approx. 96g) coarse white bulgur

2 tbsp olive oil

5 onions, peeled and finely chopped

1½ tsp pink salt

½ tsp black pepper

TO GARNISH

Extra-virgin olive oil

Spring onions, finely sliced

Radishes, finely sliced

Micro greens

METHOD

First, wash the lentils and bulgur separately with cold water.

Add the lentils to a pot, followed by enough water at room temperature to cover them, about three cups (700ml). Bring to the boil then cook for 10 minutes.

After this time, drain the lentils, saving the cooking water for later.

Meanwhile, add the olive oil to a pot over a high heat and fry the chopped onions.

Once the onions start to shrink, turn the heat down to medium-low and stir intermittently as they cook.

Once the onions are dark golden brown and caramelised, add the reserved lentil cooking water which should be about two and a half cups (about 600ml).

Add the washed bulgur, followed by the cooked lentils, salt and pepper.

Add extra water if needed to cover everything. Cover the pot with a lid and simmer on a low heat until the bulgur and lentils are fully cooked, which should take about 25 to 30 minutes.

TO SERVE

Arrange the pilaf in a large serving dish, then drizzle some extra-virgin olive oil over the top. Garnish with the spring onions, radishes and micro greens to finish.

The cooking process calms me and feeding friends and family is gratifying. I feel that this is how I express my love towards people. On the other hand, teaching people in my class is also incredibly rewarding as I am able to empower them to lead a healthier, happier life through cooking. Personally, I try to be grateful for the small things every day, and also feel that travelling breaks the routine which is key to looking after your mental health.

LAMA JAMMAL (@MAMALUKITCHEN)

TARKA DAL

PREPARATION TIME: 10 MINUTES | COOKING TIME: 50-55 MINUTES | SERVES 4-6

I wish I could say my mother cooked this dal for me (she didn't) but it is a hug in a meal that I've cooked so many times over the years, and fed to so many friends and neighbours.

INGREDIENTS

150g red lentils

150g yellow split peas

2½ litres water

35g ginger, peeled and grated

6 cloves of garlic, peeled and grated

1 whole hot small chilli (green or red)

1 tsp salt

½ tsp ground turmeric

2 tbsp ghee, coconut oil or olive oil

2 tsp black mustard seeds

1 tsp cumin seeds

10-12 fresh or dried curry leaves

2 onions, finely sliced

50g coriander, leaves and stalks

1 lemon, juiced

METHOD

Rinse the lentils and split peas in a sieve until the water runs clear, then put them into a large saucepan with the water.

Bring to the boil, skim and discard any foam, then add the ginger, garlic, chilli, salt and turmeric.

Turn down the heat and simmer the dal for around 45 minutes until creamy. You are likely to need more water, and do stir occasionally as it can stick as it thickens. You may choose to use a whisk at the end to break down some of the cooked lentils and get a creamier dal. When it's ready, the lentils should be soft.

In a large frying pan, heat the ghee or oil with the black mustard and cumin seeds on a reasonably high heat for just a few minutes. As soon as they begin to pop, turn the heat down to medium-low, add the curry leaves for a 20 second sizzle, then add the onions. Cook slowly for 8 to 10 minutes, stirring occasionally. The onions should be brown and unctuous as this will flavour the dal. Turn off the heat when they're done and set aside.

Finely chop the coriander stalks and add them to the dal a few minutes before it finishes cooking. Stir in the lemon juice and most of the tarka onions, leaving a little for garnish.

Serve the dal with fresh coriander leaves and the rest of the fried onions on top.

Over my lifetime, I have tried a long list of things in my quest for stability, self-acceptance, confidence, and a deeper understanding of life's complexities. Psychotherapy is probably top of that list, but finding a friend with whom you can have completely honest conversations, whenever you need, cannot be underrated. Permitting yourself to be in touch with all your feelings is so important. Most of us spend so much energy denying and avoiding the uncomfortable pain inside of us, but if you've had a childhood, you've most likely got wounds too, and they need your attention.

EMMA LATELY (@EMMALATELYNUTRITION)

NATURAL YOGHURT

PREPARATION TIME: 20 MINUTES, PLUS 8-12 HOURS SETTING | MAKES APPROX. 500G

I know you can buy yoghurt from a supermarket quite easily and yeah, it tastes good… but seriously, nothing beats making it yourself. It's mild and creamy but also the fruit of your labour, which makes it even more magical.

INGREDIENTS

500ml whole (preferably organic) milk
2 tbsp live natural yoghurt

EQUIPMENT

A digital thermometer
A wide-mouthed thermos flask or yoghurt maker

METHOD

Pour the milk into a fairly large saucepan and place over a medium heat. Stir occasionally to make sure it doesn't catch. Gradually heat until it's almost bubbling and reaches 87°c on your thermometer, then turn off the heat and set aside.

Allow the milk to cool to 46.5°c.

While the milk is cooling, thoroughly wash your yoghurt maker or flask and sterilise it using boiling water. Once the milk reaches the right temperature, work quickly to add the live natural yoghurt and whisk in thoroughly.

Transfer the milk mixture to your yoghurt maker or thermos flask and leave in a warm place in the house (I store mine in the airing cupboard) for at least 8 hours or overnight. It is important that the flask or pot is not moved at all during this time.

The following morning, as if by magic, you should be able to unveil a batch of beautifully silky homemade yoghurt. Store in the fridge and if your yoghurt separates after a day or so, just stir well to combine the liquids and solids again.

When approaching the end of your batch, reserve two tablespoons of yoghurt to repeat the process as above or start over.

TO SERVE

Stir through some fruit compote and scatter with nuts and seeds for a healthy breakfast or dollop onto fresh fruit salad as a light dessert. You could even blend 75g of your yoghurt with approximately 150g of frozen fruit and a dash of honey for some instant froyo!

Mental health is something I feel strongly about supporting. My advice would be this: don't compare yourself to others, it's not a race. Immerse yourself in activities that interest you, not those that carry 'worth' as viewed by society. Be open and honest about how you feel with people you can trust; never keep things to yourself. Lastly, always be kind to yourself, and to others.

STEPH BLACKWELL (@STEPHIBLACKWELL)

GUTSY MUFFINS

PREPARATION TIME: 10 MINUTES | COOKING TIME: 20 MINUTES | MAKES 12

These muffins are full of lots of different starches and indigestible fibres that feed your microbiome, and the pears add natural fruity sweetness. You can choose any additional flavours from spices to chocolate chips, but I love almond and raspberry.

INGREDIENTS

25g oats

1 x 410g tin of pear halves in juice

75g caster sugar

40g honey

40ml light olive oil

25g cooked rice

1 tsp almond extract

2 eggs

120g plain flour

50g wholemeal plain flour

10g flaxmeal

2 tsp baking powder

1 tsp cinnamon

Handful of frozen raspberries

METHOD

Preheat the oven to 180°c fan.

Make a kind of porridge by putting the oats in a small saucepan with 100ml of the juice from the tinned pears.

Simmer for 3 minutes on the lowest heat until the oats are soft. Add this 'porridge' to a blender with the pear halves, sugar, honey, oil, rice and almond extract then blend until smooth. Crack in the eggs and pulse until incorporated.

In a mixing bowl, toss together the flours, flaxmeal, baking powder and cinnamon. Pour the dry ingredients into the blender mixture and stir until combined.

Prepare a 12-hole muffin tin with paper cases. Spoon the batter into each case until a quarter full, drop two frozen raspberries into each one and then add more batter until three quarters full.

Bake the muffins in the preheated oven for 18 to 20 minutes, then leave to cool slightly before serving.

Food has the potential to cause damage to the mind and body, but also has the potential to heal, sustain and nourish. The kitchen has always been a sanctuary for me; I find the act of kneading bread or shelling nuts meditative. Making food to share with others feeds a community, which in turn feeds my life.

DAVID ATHERTON (@NOMADBAKERDAVID)

TURMERIC CHAI PROTEIN BALLS

PREPARATION TIME: 10 MINUTES, PLUS CHILLING TIME | MAKES 10

These snacks are loaded with healthy fats, protein and anti-inflammatory spices.
Turmeric positively impacts over 60 different systems in our body including gut health, brain health and detoxification.

INGREDIENTS

100g ground almonds
80g desiccated coconut
2 tsp ground turmeric
1 tsp ground cinnamon
1 tsp ground cardamom
Pinch of ground cloves
Pinch of ground black pepper
35ml (4 tbsp) coconut oil
35ml (2 tbsp) honey

METHOD

Put all the dry ingredients in a bowl (the ground almonds, desiccated coconut and spices) and mix well.

Add the coconut oil and honey to the bowl, then mix until everything is well combined.

Use your hands to make walnut-sized balls of the mixture, compressing them to make the ingredients stick.

Let the protein balls chill in the fridge for a couple of hours before enjoying.

If you have any left, keep them stored in the fridge.

Food is medicine! Turmeric, for example, is something you can incorporate into any dish to benefit from this anti-inflamamtory spice. Up to 95% of serotonin (your happy hormone) is made in the gut and so by supporting your gut health with the right kinds of foods you are also supporting your mental health. During stressful times I always try to make meals regular and nutritious, which helps me cope so much better, as it won't cause energy dips which can increase anxiety.

FARZANAH NASSER (@INSIDE.OUT.NUTRITION)

STEPHANIE GOOLD

HEALTHY GUT WAKE-UP SHAKE

PREPARATION TIME: 5 MINUTES | SERVES 1

As a nutritional therapist, I am always trying to think of ways to help my patients include more veggies in their diet. This smoothie is a tasty take on a Frappuccino™; even if you hate cauliflower, I promise you won't taste it!

INGREDIENTS

160ml coffee, cooled (use high quality beans if you can, as they contain beneficial antioxidants)

80ml milk of your choice

2 tbsp cocoa powder (or 1 scoop chocolate protein powder)

1 small banana

4 shelled walnuts

1 large handful of spinach

3 frozen cauliflower florets

3 ice cubes

METHOD

To make the shake, simply blend all the ingredients together in a high-speed blender until you have a smoothie-like consistency.

Some people find it difficult eating the recommended seven servings of vegetables and fruits per day (five veg, two fruit) but if you start the day with some at breakfast, then you'll be well on your way to achieving that goal.

Cruciferous vegetables such as cauliflower, cabbage and broccoli contain glucosinolates, known to promote anti-cancer properties and to promote liver detoxification.

They are also an excellent source of food for our gut bacteria, essential for healthy digestion, immunity and serotonin (the happy hormone) production.

Looking after your health and wellbeing can be difficult if you don't feel mentally motivated to do so, or perhaps you don't even feel worthy. However, having the right nutrition can really make a difference in supporting the health of the brain and regulating mood. As a nutritional therapist, I can understand the scientific reasons as to why eating healthily can impact my mental health. This doesn't mean I'm perfect, or have days when I feel like I can't be bothered! It's about balance and having a few easy recipes up your sleeve.

STEPHANIE GOOLD (@SUNSHINE_NUTRITION_)

"

THE KEY TO COOKING DELICIOUS FOOD
QUICKLY IS TO USE FRESH INGREDIENTS.
I LIKE TO GO SHOPPING WITHOUT
A LIST AND THEN JUST FOLLOW THE
INGREDIENTS THAT JUMP OUT AT ME.
IT NEVER FAILS TO INSPIRE ME TO COOK.

CHAPTER THREE

FAST FOOD
(BUT NOT AS YOU KNOW IT)

Fast food doesn't mean junk food, but people often confuse the two.

There are many quick, easy and healthy dishes that you can get done in less than 60 minutes without too many ingredients. Some of my favourite dishes to cook at home are those that require little time and effort.

For me, nothing is more relaxing than cooking healthy recipes that make you feel good. Sometimes I am short on time but still want to cook for myself or for family and friends. The key to cooking delicious food quickly is to use fresh ingredients.

I like to go shopping without a list and then just follow the ingredients that jump out at me. It never fails to inspire me to cook.

When I don't have much time, I turn to dishes such as tortillas with seasonal vegetables, vibrant salads with whatever takes my fancy, or a simple stew with chickpeas. A good option for making delicious yet healthy food quickly is to cook vegetables or fish a la plancha (on the grill) and then serve them with some good crusty bread.

You can't go wrong with fresh ingredients cooked simply.

José Pizarro
(@jose_pizarro)

MEXICAN BEEF & JALAPEÑO QUESADILLAS

PREPARATION TIME: 20 MINUTES | COOKING TIME: 30 MINUTES | SERVES 4

These quesadillas are always quick off the table and great with kids.
They are very filling and perfect for when you're feeding a crowd.

INGREDIENTS

2 tbsp olive oil

1 onion, peeled and diced

2 cloves of garlic, peeled and crushed

500g minced beef

2 tsp paprika

2 tsp ground cumin

1 x 400g tin of chopped tomatoes

1 x 400g tin of kidney beans, drained and rinsed

Sea salt and freshly ground black pepper

4 x 25cm tortillas

1-2 tbsp olive oil, for brushing

200g mixture of mozzarella and cheddar cheese, grated

80g pickled jalapeño chillies

4 spring onions, trimmed and sliced

Sour cream, to serve

FOR THE SALSA

4 tomatoes, diced

1 red onion, peeled and finely diced

Large handful of coriander, roughly chopped

1 lime, juiced

METHOD

Preheat the oven to 220°c or 200°c fan. Line two large baking trays with baking paper.

Place a large, non-stick frying pan over a high heat. Add the oil and onion to cook for 2 to 3 minutes, or until the onion has softened.

Add the garlic and cook for 2 minutes, then crumble in the minced beef. Cook over a high heat for 4 to 5 minutes, or until the mince is lightly browned.

Stir in the paprika and cumin then cook for 1 to 2 minutes before adding the tinned tomatoes. Cook for another 2 minutes, then remove from the heat.

Stir in the kidney beans and season to taste with salt and pepper.

Lightly brush one side of two tortillas with oil and place them on the prepared trays, oiled side down. Sprinkle both with a little of the cheeses and spread half the beef mixture over each one. Scatter the jalapeños, spring onions and remaining cheese on top.

Brush one side of the two remaining tortillas with oil and place them on top of the beef filling, oiled side up. Press them down firmly and place the quesadillas on the two highest shelves of the preheated oven for 10 to 15 minutes, or until golden brown.

While the quesadillas are cooking, mix all the salsa ingredients together in a bowl and season to taste. Remove the quesadillas from the oven and cut into wedges before serving with a dollop of sour cream and your salsa on the side.

Tip: These can be quite hot and spicy, so for a tamer dish, go easy on the jalapeños, or leave them out altogether. Making the salsa from scratch might seem like an added hassle but is definitely worth it.

*From Quick and Delicious by Gordon Ramsay

YOGHURT PIZZA

PREPARATION TIME: 10-15 MINUTES | COOKING TIME: 5-10 MINUTES | MAKES 2

Everyone loves pizza and it has so many memories attached. It's a meal where you can create any flavour you like. There is no right or wrong way. This version is really quick because the dough doesn't need to rise.

INGREDIENTS

FOR THE DOUGH

220g self-raising flour

220g Greek or soya yoghurt

½ tsp baking powder (optional)

FOR THE TOPPING

1 tin of chopped tomatoes, blended (or 1 jar of passata)

1 ball of mozzarella

METHOD

FOR THE DOUGH

Combine all the ingredients together until you have a soft dough.

Shape this into a ball and cut in half.

On a floured surface, roll each half of the dough out to the thickness of a pound coin.

You can make your own self-raising flour using half a teaspoon of baking powder to every 150g of organic bread flour, and if you prefer to use plant-based yoghurt then soya will also work.

FOR THE TOPPING

Place your pizza base into an extremely hot ovenproof frying pan, spreading it out so the dough goes up the sides of the pan to form a crust.

Cook for 1 to 2 minutes so the base gets crispy underneath, then start to add the toppings.

Make sure the tomato sauce is highly seasoned to taste, then spread a generous spoonful from the centre towards the edges in a smooth but not too thick layer.

Tear over some mozzarella and add whatever other toppings you like.

By this stage, the dough should begin to bubble up as it cooks, so place the pan under an extremely hot grill for 2 minutes until the cheese melts and the crust becomes crispy and golden.

Slide your pizza onto a board, slice it up however you like it and enjoy.

I think there are so many mental health issues in the hospitality industry, so it's about time we start talking about our issues and sharing advice with each other. For me, cooking is the perfect way to focus; it gives you the opportunity to be creative and use your mind to its full potential.

MARK TUTTIETT (@KOOZE)

HONEY & SOY VEGETABLE STIR FRY

PREPARATION TIME: 10 MINUTES | COOKING TIME: 10 MINUTES | SERVES 2

Stir fries are great meals that tick all the boxes: quick, easy, delicious, cheap and healthy.
They can be made in minutes yet are full of flavour. Use any vegetables you prefer, I have just included the commonly used ones.

INGREDIENTS

2 tbsp vegetable cooking oil

1 clove of garlic, finely chopped

1 pack of shiitake mushrooms (you can substitute other mushrooms)

1 carrot, cut into matchsticks

1 cup of sliced cabbage

1 cup of chopped broccoli

150g medium egg noodles, cooked

2 cups of beansprouts

FOR THE HONEY AND SOY SAUCE

3 tbsp soy sauce

2 tbsp honey

1 clove of garlic, minced

1 tbsp cornflour

1 tsp sesame oil

1 tsp sesame seeds

Pinch of salt and pepper

METHOD

Put all the ingredients for the honey and soy sauce into a bowl and mix until combined. Prepare all your vegetables and noodles so everything is to hand.

Put the vegetable oil into a large pan or wok on a medium heat, then add the finely chopped garlic.

Stir until the garlic turns crispy and golden, then add the mushrooms and cook for a few more minutes.

Add the vegetables in order of how long they take to cook, starting with the one that takes longest, which in this case is the carrot, then the cabbage, then the broccoli. Leave the beansprouts until the end.

Quickly stir everything on a medium heat for a few minutes then add the egg noodles and mix them with all the vegetables.

Pour in the honey and soy sauce; at this point you need to stir really quickly to coat everything and help the sauce turn nice and glossy (the cornflour helps with this).

Finally, add the beansprouts, mix well and turn the heat off. Serve immediately.

I want to encourage people to cook more at home and enjoy homemade food. Cooking brings me happiness and I find it relaxing. It also helps you to stay healthy and have a balanced lifestyle. Eat well, live well, be yourself and don't compare yourself with other people.
YUI MILES (@COOKINGWITH_YUI)

JAMES WYTHE

15 MINUTE VEGAN PAD THAI

PREPARATION TIME: 5 MINUTES | COOKING TIME: 10 MINUTES | SERVES 2

This quick and easy meal is absolutely rammed full of colour and flavour. You will be shocked that it's actually free from gluten, dairy, egg and refined sugar! If you enjoy Thai food, then you're going to absolutely love this recipe.

INGREDIENTS

2 tbsp sesame oil

1 red onion, sliced

1 large clove of garlic, finely chopped or crushed

½ a red chilli, deseeded and sliced

1 head of broccoli, sliced into small florets

1 red pepper, sliced

150g rice noodles

2 large handfuls of beansprouts

1 small handful of unsalted peanuts, crushed

1 lime, juiced

FOR THE SAUCE

1 tsp sesame oil

3 tbsp maple syrup

3 tbsp tamari

1 heaped tsp miso paste (I use brown rice miso)

METHOD

Firstly heat a pan with the sesame oil, then add the red onion, garlic and chilli and fry for a couple of minutes. Now add the broccoli and red pepper, then fry for another 5 minutes until they've softened.

Meanwhile, cook the rice noodles according to the packet instructions and prepare the sauce by mixing the sesame oil, maple syrup, tamari and miso in a small bowl until smooth.

Add most of the beansprouts to the pan along with the crushed peanuts, lime juice and your sauce. Stir everything together and cook for a couple of minutes.

Finally, add the noodles to the pan and toss them through the vegetables, letting them soak up all that sauce.

I like to serve my pad thai with the remaining crunchy beansprouts on top plus extra chopped chilli, wedges of lime and crushed peanuts for garnish. The rest will keep for lunch the next day if you are cooking for just one!

Cooking has helped me through my tough times with illness; it's been my safe place and reduces my thoughts about other areas of life. I also take part in hobbies such as golf and light exercise, which help to relieve stress for me. However, it's ok to not always be on top form. Failing is part of improving.

JAMES WYTHE (@HEALTHYLIVINGJAMES)

REBECCA LUND & KATE ARTHUR

QUICK & EASY CHICKEN LARB

PREPARATION TIME: 10 MINUTES | COOKING TIME: 25 MINUTES | SERVES 4

This recipe makes for such a fun and interactive meal with loved ones. Everyone can choose exactly how much filling they'd like in their lettuce cups and find their favourite combinations... It's fresh, flavoursome and super quick to prepare.

INGREDIENTS

1 onion, finely chopped

2 cloves of garlic, minced

3 tbsp oil

2 tbsp toasted sesame oil

800g chicken mince

15cm ginger, grated

2 red chillies, finely chopped

½ cup (approx. 125ml) hoisin sauce

¼ cup (approx. 62g) toasted sesame seeds

60g coriander, finely chopped

2 limes, juiced

¼ cup (approx. 62ml) sriracha

½ cup (approx. 125ml) mayonnaise

2 carrots, grated

2 baby marrows, grated

3 tbsp pickled ginger, finely chopped

2 tbsp pickling liquid from the ginger

Pinch of salt

4 baby gem lettuces

½ cup (approx. 125g) roasted and salted peanuts

METHOD

In a large pan, fry the onion and garlic in the oil and sesame oil until softened.

Add the chicken mince, ginger and chilli and fry until the chicken starts to brown.

Add the hoisin, sesame seeds, coriander and lime juice to the pan and cook for another 5 minutes. Meanwhile, mix the sriracha and mayonnaise together in a small bowl.

For the pickled vegetables, mix the grated carrots and baby marrows with the chopped pickled ginger in a bowl, then stir in the pickling liquid from the ginger and a pinch of salt.

When you are ready to assemble your larb, grab a lettuce leaf and fill it with the chicken mixture, sriracha mayo and gingery veg then top with crunchy peanuts. Delish!

Cooking and being in the kitchen has long been a creative outlet for us. It's something that we are passionate about and yes, it is what we wake up for in the mornings...it's given us a purpose and inspired others to do the same, and for that reason cooking has grounded us and helped us look after our mental health. We love the heart behind this project and are delighted to be involved in creating awareness about mental health, getting more people to come together, speak up and be encouraged by the fact that they aren't alone.

KATE ARTHUR & REBECCA LUND (@DELISHSISTERS)

FIRECRACKER CHICKEN POPPERS

PREPARATION TIME: 5-10 MINUTES | COOKING TIME: 5-10 MINUTES | SERVES 6-7

These make brilliant appetisers and can very happily be eaten as a main course with some fries.
I do have to tell you that they are incredibly addictive...in a faceplant-the-bowl kind of way. Consider yourself warned!

INGREDIENTS

700g chicken breast
285g breadcrumbs
Oil, for deep frying
1 lemon, cut into wedges

FOR THE CHILLI COATING

335ml sriracha or hot chilli sauce (or to taste)
85ml sweet chilli sauce (or to taste)
1 egg, beaten
½ tsp onion powder
½ tsp garlic powder

FOR THE FLOUR COATING

120g (approx. 1 cup) plain flour
1 tsp salt
1 tsp black pepper
1 tsp garlic powder
1 tsp onion powder
1 tsp chilli powder
½ tsp paprika

FOR THE DIPPING SAUCE

5 tbsp mayonnaise
3 tbsp sriracha or hot chilli sauce (or to taste)
3 tbsp sweet chilli sauce (or to taste)
½ a lime, juiced

METHOD

Mix all the ingredients for the chilli coating together in a wide, shallow bowl then set aside. Do the same for the flour coating, and pour the breadcrumbs into a separate bowl.

Lay out the bowls in this order: flour coating, chilli coating, breadcrumbs.

In a smaller bowl, combine all the ingredients for the dipping sauce and set aside.

Cut the chicken breast into bite-size pieces then toss them in the flour coating, dip them in the chilli coating, and lastly roll them in the breadcrumbs.

Place on a clean dry plate. You can store these in the fridge at this stage for several hours before you need them.

Deep fry the coated chicken pieces in oil heated to 180°c for 3 to 4 minutes, or until golden and cooked through.

You might need to do this in batches so the pan isn't crowded, as this can lower the oil temperature. They cook quickly so be careful not to burn them.

Serve hot with the wedges of lemon and the dipping sauce on the side.

I suffered from postnatal depression and cooking was the creative outlet I needed when I was struggling to cope. I started an Instagram page and gathered a large following; opportunity sprung from my really low moments and I am now pursuing dreams and passions I never thought I would or could. I also faced some big fears and won a TV cooking competition at my most vulnerable, just six weeks after I had my second baby by C-section. Your thoughts define who you are and who you become, so make sure you stay positive and be kind to yourself.

SABRINA BUTT (@SABRINAS_KITCHEN_)

WHEN I STRUGGLED WITH DEPRESSION AND
ANXIETY, I WAS LUCKY TO BE SURROUNDED BY
A LOVING FAMILY BUT STILL, REACHING OUT
FOR HELP WAS ONE OF THE BIGGEST ACTS OF
STRENGTH OF MY LIFE.

SPEAKING OUT AND SHOWING YOUR FRAGILITY IS
SOMETHING TO BE PROUD OF, NOT ASHAMED BY.

DANILO CORTELLINI
(@DANILOCORTELLINI)

HARISSA & HALLOUMI QUESADILLAS

PREPARATION TIME: 5 MINUTES | COOKING TIME: 5 MINUTES | MAKES 4

For the ultimate quick and easy lunch, these quesadillas are the answer. The harissa, a North African spice paste, adds a really punchy heat that's balanced out by the salty halloumi which cooks quickly and gives you the required ooze factor.

INGREDIENTS

250g halloumi

4 tbsp rose harissa

8 soft tortillas

Handful of finely chopped coriander leaves

4 spring onions, finely chopped

Sea salt

1 tbsp olive oil

METHOD

Using the coarse side of a box grater, shred the block of halloumi.

Lay out four of the tortillas, then spread a tablespoon of the rose harissa over each of them. Top with the cheese, coriander and spring onions. Add a pinch of salt and put the remaining tortillas on top to make four quesadillas.

Put a non-stick frying pan on a medium-high heat.

Brush the pan with a little olive oil and pop in one of the quesadillas. Cook for about 1 to 2 minutes on each side until the tortilla is golden and the cheese has melted.

Serve immediately and repeat with the remaining quesadillas.

I find cooking utterly therapeutic. It's soothing and calming and I get to eat. It's one of the few times I really switch off. Apart from cooking, exercise really helps me a lot with looking after my mental health, as well as cutting loose. Being with my mates having fun is an utter elixir and when I feel crap I often find it's the best tonic. Also, talk more. For years and years I didn't and it was a disaster. Having a conversation about how you feel should be easy, especially if you are surrounded by great people.

JOHN GREGORY-SMITH (@JOHNGS)

SPICY MIXED BEAN STEW

PREPARATION TIME: 10 MINUTES | COOKING TIME: 30-35 MINUTES | SERVES 3-4

This easy and cheap recipe freezes really well, so make a big batch when you've got the physical and mental energy for days when you have less. I like mine with grilled cheese on top and some crusty bread.

INGREDIENTS

1 large onion

3 sticks of celery

1 red pepper and 1 orange pepper (or whatever colours you have)

120g mushrooms (if you like them)

7-8cm chorizo (optional)

Oil, for frying

3 tins of beans (butter beans, kidney beans and black beans work well, but whatever you can find is fine)

2 tins of chopped tomatoes

2 tsp smoked paprika

1 tsp garlic powder

OR

1 sachet of fajita/Tex-Mex/Mexican spice mix

METHOD

Dice the vegetables (and chorizo if using) into small chunks and add to a large pan.

Fry in a little oil on a medium heat until soft.

Drain and rinse the beans then add them to the vegetables.

Stir in the smoked paprika and garlic, or the spice mix. Mix well to coat the vegetables in the seasoning, then add the chopped tomatoes and stir again.

Leave the stew to simmer for 15 to 20 minutes until the tomato sauce has thickened. Taste it before you serve up: if it's not sweet enough for you, add some barbecue sauce, and if it's lacking flavour, add more spices and some salt and pepper.

Serve on its own, with rice or with slices of crusty bread.

I have battled with anxiety and PTSD following domestic abuse. Since leaving and recovering, I prioritise my mental health. I do things every day to keep me feeling my best, including making sure I sleep well, move my body, eat well, connect with friends and take time to reflect. Professional mental health support from a charity saved my life. Charities who normalise mental health struggles are vital to the recovery of so many. Talk to people! Don't pretend to be ok when you're not. Nobody expects you to have all the answers or to get it right all the time.

SOPHIE MEDLIN (@SOPHIEDIETITIAN)

BAKED POMEGRANATE FETA WITH SPICED RED PEPPER SAUCE & TABBOULEH

PREPARATION TIME: 10 MINUTES | COOKING TIME: 20-30 MINUTES | SERVES 2

This recipe is vegetarian and gluten-free, but aside from that it's something I have cooked for years in one way or another which brings me comfort, a sense of familiarity and joy.

INGREDIENTS

FOR THE RED PEPPER SAUCE

150g baby plum tomatoes

100g roasted jarred red peppers

3 cloves of garlic, kept in their skins

1 red chilli, stalk removed

½ a red onion, cut into wedges

1 tsp ras el hanout

Olive oil

Salt and pepper

FOR THE FETA

200g feta

1 tbsp pomegranate molasses

1 tsp za'atar

1 tsp runny honey

FOR THE TABBOULEH

100g quinoa (mixed, white or red)

30g flat leaf parsley, finely chopped

30g fresh coriander, finely chopped

15g mint, stalks removed, finely chopped

75g baby plum tomatoes, finely chopped

½ a red onion, finely chopped

½ a lemon, juiced

METHOD

Preheat your oven to 220°c fan.

Meanwhile, cook the quinoa for the tabbouleh according to the packet instructions, then drain it and leave to cool (unless you are using pre-cooked quinoa).

Place all the ingredients for the red pepper sauce onto a medium-size baking tray, sprinkling the ras el hanout evenly over everything.

Drizzle with olive oil (about two tablespoons) then season with salt and pepper. Place the tray in the preheated oven to roast the vegetables for 20 minutes until charred and soft.

Meanwhile, line a small baking tray with tin foil or baking parchment then place the block of feta on top. Drizzle with the pomegranate molasses, za'atar and a tablespoon of olive oil. Place in the hot oven to cook for 15 minutes until soft and golden.

Place the cooked and cooled quinoa, parsley, coriander, mint, chopped baby tomatoes and chopped onion into a mixing bowl.

Add two tablespoons of olive oil and the lemon juice, season with salt and pepper and toss everything together to make the tabbouleh.

Remove the roasted vegetables from the oven, take out the whole garlic cloves and squeeze the soft garlic out of the skins into a food processor along with the rest of the roasted vegetables. Blend until smooth to make the red pepper sauce.

Divide the tabbouleh between plates. Remove the feta from the oven and drizzle with honey. Place the baked feta on top of the tabbouleh, along with any juices from the tray then spoon over some of the spiced red pepper sauce.

I often struggle with anxiety and I've learnt to listen to my body when I feel it coming on. I learnt that it's okay to say no to people if you are not feeling yourself; there is no shame in that. If I'm not feeling particularly great, I make sure to nourish my body with food that will give me energy, try to up my exercise for that week, cut out coffee for a while to help tackle anxious feelings and take time for myself with long candlelit baths and comfort food.

LIBERTY FENNELL (@LIBERTYFENNELL)

TANDOORI SEA BASS & BOMBAY POTATOES

PREPARATION TIME: 10 MINUTES | COOKING TIME: 15 MINUTES | SERVES 4

My boys absolutely devour this; it's a great family meal as there is very little heat in the tandoori masala, and the Bombay potatoes are packed full of nutritious veggies. It's a really quick and easy midweek option too!

INGREDIENTS

FOR THE BOMBAY POTATOES

700-750g cooked new potatoes

1½ tsp cumin seeds

1 tsp black mustard seeds

1 large white onion, finely sliced into half moons

3 small cloves of garlic, grated

2.5cm ginger, grated

Fresh chillies, to taste

1½ tsp coriander seeds, toasted and ground

1½ tsp garam masala

½ tsp ground turmeric

1½ tsp Maldon sea salt (or to taste)

12-15 baby plum tomatoes, halved

40g butter

80-100g baby leaf spinach

Fresh coriander, leaves chopped

FOR THE TANDOORI SEA BASS

⅓ tsp each garlic granules and fennel seeds

½ tsp each ground turmeric and Kashmiri chilli powder

1 tsp each garam masala, ground cumin and ground coriander

1-1½ tsp Maldon sea salt

4 boneless sea bass fillets, skin on

1 lemon, zested

METHOD

FOR THE BOMBAY POTATOES

To prepare your potatoes, cut new potatoes into bite-size pieces and keep the skin on when boiling. If using standard potatoes, peel and cut into bite-size pieces before boiling.

Fry the cumin and mustard seeds in a little vegetable oil until they start to crackle, then add the sliced onion. Once softened, add the garlic, ginger and chillies. Allow everything to take on a golden colour, then add the ground spices and salt.

Cook for a bit but don't let the spices burn, adding a splash of water if needed.

Now add the tomatoes and allow them to break down into a sauce. Add about 100ml of water at this point and let it all reduce. Once you have a thick, unctuous sauce, test the seasoning and adjust as necessary. Stir in the cooked potatoes and mix well. I like to mash a couple of the potatoes into the sauce for different textures. This is also the point to add your butter.

Finally, stir in the spinach and allow it to wilt. You may need a touch more water here. Sprinkle the Bombay potatoes with some chopped coriander to finish.

FOR THE TANDOORI SEA BASS

Mix the garlic, fennel, turmeric, chilli powder, garam masala, cumin, coriander and salt together. Lightly oil the sea bass fillets on both sides and sprinkle the tandoori masala spice mix on the flesh side only, along with some lemon zest and a touch of salt.

Fry in a medium-hot pan, skin side down, until almost cooked through, then flip to the flesh side for the last minute. This is so the spice coating doesn't burn.

Assemble your dish and serve the tandoori seabass and Bombay potatoes with mint raita and wedges of lemon for squeezing over.

Cooking has always been my happy place, and my kitchen is my sanctuary. It's through food that I connect with not only myself, but the ones I love and feed. It's an expression of emotion as well as nourishment; I feel you can taste the love. I think mental health and wellbeing needs to be put on a par with physical health and wellbeing; to me the two are inextricably linked. We need to have this 360 degree approach.

SARAH WOODS (@MYHOMECOOKEDUK)

TRUFFLED ARTICHOKES, PARMESAN & LEMON

PREPARATION TIME: 5 MINUTES | COOKING TIME: LESS THAN 5 MINUTES | SERVES 2

If you can, create a reason to make and devour this incredible plateful! It's an antipasti-style modern Italian dish, ideal for enjoying in the garden or with friends any night of the week. I just love the flavour profile celebrated here.

INGREDIENTS

1 tbsp olive oil

2 tbsp white truffle oil

2 tbsp aged balsamic vinegar

300g pickled or jarred artichokes, drained and quartered

50g great quality parmesan

Sea salt, to taste

Cracked black pepper, to taste

METHOD

Whisk the oils and balsamic vinegar together in a small bowl.

Heat a frying pan and dry fry the artichokes for 1 minute on each side. It's very important not to shake them around at this stage because we want the artichokes to toast.

Arrange the warm artichokes on a serving plate of your choice, drizzle over the truffle and balsamic dressing, finely grate the parmesan over the top and finish with a generous pinch of salt and pepper. Enjoy!

Cooking has helped me to look after my mental health because creating a gift to be appreciated by yourself or others will attract a sense of achievement and self-worth. It also stimulates the mind with focus and ambition. "Feeling Good, Cooking Better" is my thinking phrase when times get tough in life and work, to keep me focused and humble.

RYAN STAFFORD (@RYANCHEFSTAFFORD)

PRAWN MOILEE

PREPARATION TIME: 5 MINUTES | COOKING TIME: APPROX. 45 MINUTES | SERVES 4

This is chef Naved Nasir's special dish at Dishoom Covent Garden. It's a light, fragrant and utterly delicious south Indian style curry, packed with juicy prawns and tempered with coconut milk. Although it looks impressive, it's very easy to make.

INGREDIENTS

55ml vegetable oil
2 tsp mustard seeds
30 fresh curry leaves
300g white onions
15g garlic paste
15g ginger paste
2 tsp fine sea salt
1 tsp freshly ground black pepper
1¼ tsp ground turmeric
6 green chillies
25g fresh root ginger
400ml coconut milk
250ml coconut cream
300g medium tomatoes
24 large prawns
1 lemon, cut into wedges

METHOD

Remove and discard the stalks from the chillies, then slice each one into three or four long strips. Cut the white onions into chunky slices and the fresh ginger into matchsticks.

Place a large saucepan over a medium heat. Add 40ml of the oil, let it warm for a few seconds, then add the mustard seeds and 20 of the curry leaves. Let them crackle for a few seconds then add the onions and saute lightly for 12 to 14 minutes, until soft but not coloured.

Add the garlic and ginger pastes, salt, black pepper and turmeric then saute for 3 minutes, stirring regularly. Add the sliced chillies and ginger matchsticks and cook for another 3 minutes.

Pour in the coconut milk and cream then simmer for 20 minutes, stirring occasionally. If you like, you can cool and refrigerate the sauce at this stage, then reheat and continue cooking as below for an even quicker future dinner.

While the curry is simmering, place a small frying pan over a medium-high heat and add the remaining oil. Toss in the rest of the curry leaves and fry for 1 minute, until crisp. Drain on kitchen paper and set aside. Cut the tomatoes into small bite-size wedges.

Add the tomatoes and prawns to the sauce and simmer gently for a further 5 to 6 minutes, until the prawns are cooked, but do not overcook or they will be tough.

Serve the curry scattered with the fried curry leaves, with lemon wedges on the side. We also serve it with idiyappam, the white lacy noodle pancakes also known as string hoppers. If you can't get these, it goes just as well with steamed rice.

*Extract taken from Dishoom by Shamil Thakrar, Kavi Thakrar & Naved Nasir (Bloomsbury)

AT A TIME IN MY LIFE WHEN I WAS BEING
QUITE HARSH ON MYSELF, SOMEONE ASKED ME
WHETHER I WOULD SAY WHAT I WAS SAYING
TO MYSELF TO MY BEST FRIEND.

OF COURSE I SAID I WOULD NEVER.

I REALISED WE SPEND MORE TIME WITH OURSELVES
THAN ANYONE ELSE, SO REALLY, WE SHOULD BE
OUR OWN BEST FRIENDS. I TRY TO BE A LOT MORE
KIND AND FORGIVING TO MYSELF NOW.

SAFIA SHAKARCHI
(@DEARSAFIA)

HERB CRUSTED COD

PREPARATION TIME: 10 MINUTES | COOKING TIME: 10 MINUTES | SERVES 4

Simplicity itself: a delicious, sustainably sourced, herb crusted cod served with fried polenta and roasted vine tomatoes.
If you can't find sustainably sourced cod, any good quality white fish fillet or salmon will work.

INGREDIENTS

150g fresh breadcrumbs

Pinch of chilli flakes

1 clove of garlic, crushed

1 sprig of fresh parsley, chopped

30ml olive oil

Salt and pepper

500g cod fillets (about 4)

4 vines of small cherry tomatoes

500g block of pre-cooked polenta

1 sprig of fresh thyme

METHOD

Preheat the oven to 200°c fan.

In a mixing bowl, combine the breadcrumbs, chilli flakes, garlic, parsley and most of the olive oil with a pinch of salt and pepper.

Divide this equally between the fillets of fish, patting the crust down on top to hold it in place.

Place the fish on a baking tray lined with parchment along with the vine tomatoes. Drizzle a little olive oil over the tomatoes, season with salt and pepper and place the baking tray into the preheated oven for 10 minutes, or until the fish is cooked through.

While the fish and tomatoes are cooking, slice the pre-cooked polenta lengthways into four equal slabs. Fry in a hot pan with a splash of olive oil and the sprig of thyme for a couple of minutes on each side, until warmed through and slightly coloured.

To assemble the dish, place the herb crusted cod onto four plates, lay a slab of polenta next to each fillet and a vine of cherry tomatoes on top of the polenta.

Mental health awareness is a subject close to my heart and I hope this project will shine a light on those dark moments when people need it most. I try to stay positive, seeking the good in situations and only focusing on things I can control. Concentrating on anything out of your control is a thankless task; don't waste your time or headspace on it. The art of cooking, irrespective of how simple or complex, is a moment to escape in the process of creation, but importantly, it's never really about the food; it's about savouring the soul-nourishing experience of sharing it with others.

THEO MICHAELS (@THEOCOOKS)

SPAGHETTI VONGOLE

PREPARATION TIME: 30 MINUTES | COOKING TIME: 25 MINUTES | SERVES 2

I love this dish: it's quick, healthy and delicious. When my wife and I were in Italy a few years ago I ordered this every other night. If you can't get clams it works just as well with prawns or crab.

INGREDIENTS

500g clams
200g dried spaghetti
2 tbsp extra-virgin olive oil
2 cloves of garlic
½ a red chilli
Pinch of salt and pepper
6 cherry tomatoes
100ml white wine
Small bunch of flat leaf parsley

METHOD

Clean the clams in advance of cooking this dish. Submerge them in salty water for 20 minutes so that they filter out any sand and grit. Then wash in fresh cold water for 10 minutes to remove any excess salt they may have absorbed. Discard any that won't close or are broken.

When you're ready to cook, put a large pan of salted water on to boil. Meanwhile, thinly slice the garlic, finely chop the chilli and parsley and halve the tomatoes.

Once the water is boiling rapidly, add the spaghetti. Cook according to the instructions on the packet until al dente.

When the pasta has around 5 or 6 minutes left, pour the olive oil into a hot pan and add the garlic and chilli with a pinch of salt and pepper. Saute for a couple of minutes without colouring the garlic, then add the tomatoes and cleaned clams.

Pour in the white wine and cover with a lid for 3 to 4 minutes. Shake the pan every now and then. Remove the lid and discard any clams that won't open.

The pasta should now be almost ready. Check a piece; it should have a slight bite. When it's ready, drain the pasta, keeping a cup of the cooking water.

Pour the pasta into the pan of clams, add the parsley and pour in a little of the pasta water.

Keep stirring everything together over a medium heat. The starchy water should emulsify with the olive oil and coat the pasta.

TO SERVE

Use tongs to evenly distribute the spaghetti vongole between two bowls. Serve with crusty bread to mop up the sauce, and a crisp white wine.

I think mental health is a very important topic, particularly in the hospitality industry. Cooking certainly helps me relax. It's incredibly satisfying. I find exercise helps a lot too; running helps me release any built up stress.

TOM FRASER (@CHEFTOMFRASER)

JOANNA KEOHANE

LEMONY KING PRAWNS WITH GARLIC BUTTER, CHERRY TOMATOES & COURGETTI

PREPARATION TIME: 5 MINUTES | COOKING TIME: 10 MINUTES | SERVES 4

This is a great lower carb weeknight dinner which requires very little effort and just six ingredients. Rejoice: you don't even have to get a chopping board out as there's no chopping required, and it all comes together in under 20 minutes!

INGREDIENTS

2 tbsp butter
Sea salt and black pepper
500g king prawns
1 clove of garlic, peeled and crushed
½ a lemon, juiced
1 punnet of cherry tomatoes, halved
2 large courgettes, spiralised
Basil leaves (optional)

METHOD

Heat a medium skillet or frying pan with the butter in, then season the king prawns and cook them in the melted butter for about 2 to 3 minutes until they turn opaque, which means they're cooked.

Gently stir in the garlic and lemon juice, then transfer the prawns onto a plate.

In the same pan, cook the cherry tomatoes for about 5 minutes until they are starting to burst open, then transfer them to the same plate as the prawns.

Now add the spiralised courgette noodles to the pan and cook for about 2 minutes.

Place the prawns, tomatoes and all the juices on the plate back in the pan to reheat for a minute or so.

Taste the mixture and season if needed, adding more lemon juice or butter if desired.

Serve immediately and scatter some fresh basil leaves on top if you like.

Cooking for me has a twofold benefit; firstly it helps make sure that I give my body the nutrients it needs to stay healthy. But when I get into the cooking flow, it also gives me meditative time which can be a welcome break from busy life. Taking care of your mental health is absolutely key. Be kind to yourself and others. Explore what works for you, and any work you do to better understand and manage your feelings will be paid back many times over.

JOANNA KEOHANE (@JOANNAKEOHANEFOOD)

RED LENTIL HUMMUS & SEASONAL VEGETABLES

PREPARATION TIME: 15 MINUTES | COOKING TIME: 15 MINUTES | SERVES 6

I love to serve this dish as a sharing plate in the middle of the table, with some khobez (Arabic flatbreads), maybe a few salad leaves and something from the barbecue for the full experience.

INGREDIENTS

FOR THE HUMMUS

200g red lentils, washed

2g fennel seeds

60g cooked chickpeas

75g tahini

½ lemon, juiced

1 clove of garlic, peeled and finely chopped

1 tsp ground cumin

70ml good olive oil

Salt and cracked black pepper

FOR THE VEGETABLES

100g broccoli florets

8 asparagus spears, base snapped off

70g cavolo nero, washed and stalks removed

50g fresh or frozen peas

60g carrots, grated

½ a cucumber, washed and thickly sliced

2 green apples, cored, peeled and quartered

FOR THE GARNISH

30g pumpkin seeds

30g sunflower seeds

20g linseeds

1 tsp sumac

1 lemon

METHOD

FOR THE HUMMUS

Place the red lentils into a pan, cover with cold water and add a pinch of salt. Cook over a low heat for about 14 to 16 minutes, then drain and cool. Meanwhile, toast the fennel seeds in a hot dry pan for 1 minute.

Put the cooked lentils, chickpeas, tahini, lemon juice, garlic, cumin, fennel seeds and olive oil into a bowl or food processor. Blend for a good minute or so then add salt and black pepper to taste. At this stage the mixture can be 'let down' with a little warm water if it is very thick. Blend for a further 30 seconds until smooth. Spoon the hummus into a bowl, taste again to check the seasoning, cover and chill.

FOR THE VEGETABLES

Bring a pan of well-salted water to the boil, add the broccoli, cook for about 30 seconds, then drop in the asparagus and cavolo nero. Cook for a further 30 seconds, then add the peas and cook for a final 45 seconds. Drain the vegetables then place them in a bowl of iced water to cool. Transfer onto kitchen paper to dry off. Halve the asparagus spears lengthways and cut the cavolo nero leaves into smaller pieces.

FOR THE GARNISH

Roast the seeds in a hot oven for 10 to 15 minutes, then transfer them into a bowl and stir in the sumac with a touch of olive oil.

TO SERVE

Spoon the hummus onto a serving plate then evenly distribute the cooked vegetables, carrot, cucumber and apple around it. Finish with the roasted seeds, a sprinkle of sumac, a drizzle of olive oil and a good grating of lemon zest.

Sharing a plate of food at mealtimes, no matter how small, is a great way of communicating for adults and children which usually opens up the door to other topics and feelings that may have come up that day. Cooking with my mum from an early age, I remember the smells of baking, the aromas of a soup bubbling away and the taste of a freshly baked loaf of bread. The kitchen is a beautiful environment full of creativity and excitement, and cooking still gives me so much confidence and provides a great routine too.

ANDREW ASTON (@ASTON_ANDREW)

HENRY DIMBLEBY

FLASH FRIED COURGETTES WITH GREEN SAUCE

PREPARATION TIME: 5 MINUTES | COOKING TIME: 5 MINUTES | SERVES 4

This recipe is so quick to prepare and cook, and a lovely way to use up a glut of late summer courgettes. You can vary the herbs in the green sauce according to your preference too.

INGREDIENTS

FOR THE GREEN SAUCE

Handful of fresh mint (approx. 20g)

Handful of fresh flat leaf parsley (approx. 20g)

Handful of fresh coriander (approx. 20g)

1 tbsp capers

2 tsp Dijon mustard

4 anchovy fillets

200ml extra-virgin olive oil

½ a lemon, juiced

Sea salt and freshly ground black pepper

FOR THE COURGETTES

700g courgettes

3 cloves of garlic

4 tbsp extra-virgin olive oil

METHOD

FOR THE GREEN SAUCE

Put all the ingredients into a blender and blend until smooth. The sauce should be runny but substantial. Transfer into a sealable jar and pop into the fridge.

You can omit the anchovies if you need to, but they do give the sauce a rich depth. You can use any soft green herbs you have to hand; basil and tarragon both work well.

FOR THE COURGETTES

Cut the courgettes on the diagonal about 1cm thick and finely chop the garlic.

Heat the olive oil in a large heavy-bottomed frying pan. Add the courgettes, and cook fast until they start to brown (about 4 minutes).

Add the garlic 1 minute before serving, toss vigorously and season well.

Serve the flash fried courgettes immediately, drizzled with the green sauce.

*From Leon: Naturally Fast Food by Henry Dimbleby and John Vincent

Cooking is a wonderful way to clear the mind. For me it is a form of meditation. It gives you just enough to think about to make it impossible to think about anything else. It is also a wonderful way to spend time with children, particularly boys, side by side rather than face to face, allowing them to talk about what is on their minds.

HENRY DIMBLEBY (@LEONRESTAURANTS)

BOURBON BBQ TURKEY TARRAGON BURGER

PREPARATION TIME: 15 MINUTES | COOKING TIME: APPROX. 30 MINUTES | SERVES 4

This is my weekday treat: my best-ever turkey burger with bourbon barbecue sauce.
Using lean turkey mince means it's a relatively healthy option too.

INGREDIENTS

FOR THE BOURBON BBQ SAUCE

1 banana shallot, peeled
2 cloves of garlic, crushed
1 red chilli, stalk removed
2 tbsp oil
50ml bourbon
100ml pineapple juice
350g tomato ketchup
75g soft brown sugar
3 tbsp Worcestershire sauce
3 tbsp balsamic vinegar
Dash of Tabasco

FOR THE BURGERS

500g lean turkey mince
2 tbsp finely chopped tarragon
2 tsp smoked paprika
Sea salt and black pepper

FOR THE GARNISH

4 brioche burger buns
1 avocado
1 red onion
1 beef tomato
A few gherkins

METHOD

FOR THE BOURBON BBQ SAUCE

In a food processor, blitz the shallot, garlic and chilli into a paste.

Saute this paste with the oil in a medium-hot frying pan.

Once the paste has softened, add the bourbon and pineapple juice then reduce for 2 minutes before adding the remaining ingredients.

Cook the sauce until thickened to your liking, then set aside to cool.

FOR THE BURGERS

In a mixing bowl, combine the turkey mince with the tarragon, paprika, seasoning and two tablespoons of your bourbon barbecue sauce.

Using wet hands, divide the mixture into four equal amounts and roll each piece into a ball, then flatten to make a patty.

Add some oil to a hot frying pan or griddle, add the patties and cook until browned on both sides. This should take around 10 to 12 minutes in total.

When they are almost done, add enough bourbon barbecue sauce to the pan to glaze the burgers, then assemble immediately.

FOR THE GARNISH

While the burgers are cooking, slice the brioche buns open then toast them on the cut side only.

Halve and destone the avocado, then thinly slice the flesh. Cut very thin rings of red onion and thick rounds of beef tomato. Slice the gherkins.

Layer the glazed turkey burgers with all the garnishes between the toasted brioche buns and serve immediately.

15 MINUTE RAMEN

PREPARATION TIME: 5 MINUTES (WHILE COOKING) | COOKING TIME: 15 MINUTES | SERVES 1

This is one of many recipes I've shared with clients to boost their plant-based intake and get them experimenting in the kitchen. Eating well doesn't need to be expensive or complicated, and can really impact our mental health positively.

INGREDIENTS

½ a packet of smoked tofu

1 egg

1 packet of ramen noodles

Vegetables such as baby sweetcorn, mangetout, broccoli, spring onion

Sesame seeds

METHOD

Preheat the oven to 180°c fan.

Cut the tofu into squares, place on a baking tray and bake in the oven for 15 minutes. During this time, prepare the rest of the ingredients.

To soft boil the egg, place it in a pan of cold water over a medium heat and set a timer for 10 minutes.

Steam your vegetables of choice at the same time, over the water used to boil your egg, until just tender.

When the egg timer is up, run the soft boiled egg under cold water immediately and peel off the shell.

Cook the ramen noodles as per the instructions on the packet and pour them into a bowl.

Place all your vegetables into your ramen bowl. Top with baked tofu and slices of soft-boiled egg. Sprinkle with sesame seeds then enjoy.

It's so important to talk about mental health and raise its profile. I'm passionate about the way food can impact our mental health in a positive way by eating a diet rich in plant-based foods. Eating healthy does not need to be complicated or expensive. As well as cooking, I love practicing yoga and maintaining good social connections to relax and look after myself.

KAITLIN COLUCCI (@THEMISSIONDIETITIAN)

"FOOD IS PERSONAL TO EVERYONE;
IT CAN BE NOSTALGIC OR MAGICAL,
EVERYTHING OR ESSENTIAL;
IT BRINGS PEOPLE TOGETHER,
AND GIVES PLEASURE TO THE
SENSES AND THE SOUL.

CHAPTER FOUR

SOUL FOOD

We are all in search of the perfect meal. For some it can be found in a favourite restaurant, or at home with their family; for others it's the simple pleasures like a burger and a beer on a beach somewhere. Still, it's the comfort that touches your soul, that moment when the food reaches your lips and triggers those emotions.

Picture your favourite meal, feel all the joy that accompanied that meal. Just the thought of that brings back such fond memories, the taste, the smells, the conversation.

Food is personal to everyone; it can be nostalgic or magical, everything or essential; it brings people together, and gives pleasure to the senses and the soul. Our relationship with food and the emotions it can stir continues in our everyday life.

I hope the recipes in this chapter, including my play on a simple Chicken Kiev, can help bring back some of those nostalgic memories for you.

Tom Cenci
(@tomcenci)

POMEGRANATE BRAISED SHORT RIBS

PREPARATION TIME: 20 MINUTES, PLUS MARINATING OVERNIGHT | COOKING TIME: 4 HOURS | SERVES 4-6

This sweet and savoury falling-off-the-bone meat is true comfort food for me. My Syrian mother used a lot of pomegranate in her cooking, but I love Korean flavours so this recipe is a bit of both worlds.

INGREDIENTS

FOR THE RIBS

70ml pomegranate molasses

4 tbsp soy sauce

2 tbsp brown sugar

2 tbsp honey

4 cloves of garlic, minced (1 tbsp)

6 short ribs with bones (about 1.4-1.8kg)

Salt and pepper

2 tbsp olive oil

650ml beef stock

FOR THE GLAZE AND GARNISH

2 tbsp pomegranate molasses

1-2 tsp soy sauce

1 tbsp toasted sesame seeds

1 tbsp pomegranate seeds

METHOD

FOR THE RIBS

In a large bowl or ziplock bag, combine the pomegranate molasses, soy sauce, sugar, honey and garlic. Add the short ribs, toss to coat and place in the fridge overnight.

Preheat the oven to 160°c and remove the marinated short ribs from the fridge. Season with salt and pepper. Heat the olive oil in a cast iron pot or ovenproof dish, big enough to hold the short ribs in a single layer, over a medium-high heat.

Brown the ribs on all sides, approximately 3 to 4 minutes per side. Add enough stock to just cover the ribs and bring to a simmer. Cover the pot and place it in the preheated oven.

Leave the ribs to braise, checking them after 45 minutes to make sure that they are still submerged in stock, adding more if needed.

Turn the ribs and continue cooking until the meat is meltingly tender and almost falling off the bone, a total time of 3 to 3 and a half hours.

Once they are ready, remove the ribs from the cooking liquid and place them on a serving plate.

FOR THE GLAZE AND GARNISH

Make the glaze by whisking the pomegranate molasses and soy sauce into the cooking liquid left in the pot.

Pour this over the ribs, sprinkle them with the sesame and pomegranate seeds then serve with plain rice or noodles on the side.

Cooking has been therapeutic for me since I was young. It's real 'me time' where my mind only focuses on what I am preparing, and I am in the moment. If I could give my younger self some advice about mental health, it would be that self-care should be a constant effort. You may think you are alright, but if you do not look after your mental health regularly it may cause more serious issues in the long run. I try to acknowledge and share emotions I am having with those close to me, and have also started meditation.

DALIA DOGMOCH SOUBRA (@DALIASKITCHEN)

ARABIC SPICED ROAST CHICKEN

PREPARATION TIME: 15 MINUTES | COOKING TIME: 1 HOUR 15 MINUTES | SERVES 3-4

When it comes to simple one-pot meals, this tops my list of favourite fuss-free recipes. You could even prep and refrigerate everything the night before, so that it's ready for the oven an hour before dinner needs to be served.

INGREDIENTS

1 large whole chicken (approx. 1.2kg)
4 red onions, quartered
4 carrots, cut into chunks
4 potatoes, cut into chunks
2 bulbs of garlic

FOR THE MARINADE

3 tbsp olive oil
1 tsp salt
½ tsp ground black pepper
2 tbsp tomato paste
1 tsp minced ginger
1 tsp minced garlic
1 tsp ground cinnamon
¼ tsp ground cardamom
1 lemon, juiced

METHOD

Preheat the oven to 250°c fan.

FOR THE MARINADE

Mix the olive oil, salt, black pepper, tomato paste, ginger, garlic, cinnamon, cardamom and lemon juice together in a small bowl.

FOR THE CHICKEN

Thoroughly wash the chicken and pat dry, then lightly season with salt.

Place the onions, carrots, potatoes and whole garlic bulbs into a large Dutch oven (or a large ovenproof cooking pot) with the chicken, then generously coat the chicken and vegetables with the marinade.

Cover the pot with a lid, place in the preheated oven and roast the chicken and vegetables for 15 minutes.

Reduce the oven temperature to 170°c fan and leave to cook for an additional 60 minutes. In the final 15 minutes, remove the lid and allow the chicken to brown.

Serve with a fresh green salad.

Shortly after my third child was born, having been diagnosed with thyroid cancer, I had a thyroidectomy and radiation treatment followed by two weeks of self-isolation. When I returned home, life suddenly got super hectic: I had a new baby, I was dealing with post-traumatic stress and we were moving house. I don't think I realised it then, but I was slowly sinking into a depression and needed to find a way out. My husband and sister stepped in to help, knowing that food was my therapy: I would enter the kitchen, start cooking and slowly begin to heal.

ZAHRA ABDALLA (@COOKINGWITHZAHRA)

POTATO & PEA SAMOSAS

PREPARATION TIME: APPROX. 1 HOUR 30 MINUTES | COOKING TIME: APPROX. 1 HOUR | MAKES 14-16

I grew up in India, so for me street food played a huge part in those years.
When I moved to the UK I missed my friends, so I started cooking and creating the flavours of my childhood.

INGREDIENTS

FOR THE PASTRY

250g plain flour, plus extra for dusting

6 tsp sunflower oil

½ tsp salt

1 tsp ajwain seeds (caraway seeds)

100-120ml room temperature water

FOR THE FILLING

4 medium potatoes, peeled and diced small

6 tsp sunflower oil, plus extra for deep frying

1 tsp crushed fennel seeds

1 tsp cumin seeds

70g peas

1 tsp grated ginger

2-3 green chillies, finely chopped with seeds (or use 1 tsp chilli powder)

2 tsp ground coriander

1 tsp ground cumin

1 tsp mango powder

1 tsp salt

Handful of fresh coriander, chopped

METHOD

FOR THE PASTRY

Sieve the flour into a bowl, add the oil and salt, then rub the mixture together with your hands. Add the ajwain seeds and slowly pour in the water as you bring the dough together. Depending on the quality of flour, you might need less or more water.

Knead the pastry briefly until it forms a ball. It should be smooth and soft.

Cover the bowl with a cloth and leave to rest at room temperature for 1 hour.

FOR THE FILLING

Boil the diced potato in water until soft but not mushy, then drain and set aside to cool. Heat the oil in a frying pan, add the fennel and cumin seeds, then once they start sizzling add the peas and cook for a few minutes.

Stir in the grated ginger, green chilli, ground coriander, ground cumin and mango powder. Cook for 1 minute, then add the cooked potatoes to the pan, mix well and cook for 2 to 3 minutes. Add the salt and chopped coriander then continue cooking for 2 to 3 minutes on a low heat. The vegetables should be well coated with spices. Check the seasoning, then remove the pan from the heat and leave to cool.

TO MAKE THE SAMOSAS

Place a frying pan on a very low heat. Meanwhile, divide the rested pastry into seven or eight equally sized balls. On a lightly floured work surface, roll out each ball into a circle approximately 15cm in diameter. One at a time, lay the pastry circles into the frying pan to warm through (without cooking) then cut them in half.

Brush the edges of the pastry case with water. Bring the straight edges together to make a cone shape and spoon in some of the potato and pea filling. Pinch the open edge together and then press it with a fork to seal.

Repeat until all the remaining pastry pieces are made into samosas.

Heat a deep heavy-bottomed pan, half fill it with oil and bring the temperature to 180°c. Deep fry the samosas, two at a time, for 4 to 5 minutes until light brown and crisp. Lay them on kitchen paper to absorb the excess oil and fry the rest in batches. Serve the samosas with chutney or ketchup.

Food is very important for all of us. Cooking helped me not only mentally but physically. It gave me hope and through that I was able to help others. I have two teenage daughters, and I have always made sure they have balanced meals. If they want junk food they have to exercise! I run or walk every day too. I guess I have bad and good days now, but mentally I am the strongest I have ever been.

ROMY GILL (@ROMYGILL)

KOREAN-STYLE PORK TENDERLOIN

PREPARATION TIME: 30 MINUTES, PLUS MARINATING | COOKING TIME: 30 MINUTES | SERVES 4

The gentle heat of the marinade on this pork contrasts brilliantly with the cool, crunchy, pickled cucumber.
The longer you leave the meat, the more flavour it will absorb from the marinade.

INGREDIENTS

2 whole pork tenderloins or fillets

1 cucumber

1 red chilli, finely chopped

3 tbsp white wine vinegar

½ tsp caster sugar

2 tbsp sesame seeds

2-3 spring onions, sliced

1 lime, cut into wedges

FOR THE MARINADE

2 tbsp ketchup

2 tbsp soy sauce

1 tbsp sesame oil

1 tbsp honey

2 cloves of garlic, crushed

2 tsp grated ginger

2 tsp Worcestershire sauce

1-2 tsp sriracha or 1 chilli, finely chopped

METHOD

Mix all the ingredients for the marinade together in a large bowl.

Pat the pork dry with kitchen roll and lay it into the marinade. Cover and leave for 30 minutes or overnight if you have time.

Meanwhile, shave the cucumber into ribbons and pat dry with kitchen roll.

Add to a bowl, season and toss with the chilli, white wine vinegar and caster sugar to make a quick pickle.

When you're ready to cook, preheat the oven to 210°c.

Place the marinated pork fillets on a baking tray, season generously and sprinkle the sesame seeds over them (saving a few) then drizzle with oil.

Roast in the preheated oven for 25 to 30 minutes, then remove and rest for 15 minutes before carving.

Serve the pork on a platter alongside the pickled cucumber and sprinkle with the sliced spring onion, remaining sesame seeds and wedges of lime for squeezing over the top.

I love sharing my recipes and it's even better when it's for a good cause! For me, cooking is a great way to escape. I also find that regular exercise really helps with my head.
MANDY SIMMONDS (@SIMPLYFOODBYMANDY)

TAHINI CHICKEN SCHNITZEL

PREPARATION TIME: 15 MINUTES | COOKING TIME: 50 MINUTES | SERVES 4

This may sound an unlikely combination, but nutty tahini brings rich creaminess to crisp schnitzel.
Serve with a green salad or a more traditional potato salad, if you prefer.

INGREDIENTS

2 shallots, peeled and sliced into very thin rounds (90g net weight)

1 tbsp lemon juice

Salt and black pepper

2 large eggs

80g good quality tahini

2 tbsp Dijon mustard

130g panko breadcrumbs

50g sesame seeds

50g plain flour

4 large skinless chicken breasts (680g net weight)

300ml sunflower oil, for frying

FOR THE DRESSING

60g good quality tahini

2 tbsp lemon juice

1½ tbsp Dijon mustard

1 clove of garlic, peeled and crushed

2-3 tbsp finely chopped parsley leaves

METHOD

Preheat the oven to 240°c fan.

Put the shallot, lemon juice and an eighth of a teaspoon of salt in a small bowl, toss to combine, then leave to soften while you make the rest of the dish.

Whisk all the dressing ingredients in a small bowl with 50ml of water and a quarter teaspoon of salt until smooth.

Whisk the eggs, tahini, mustard, a quarter teaspoon of salt and a tablespoon of water in a shallow container (or on a plate with a lip).

In a separate container (or plate), mix the panko, sesame and a teaspoon of salt. Put the flour on a third plate.

Lay the chicken breasts on a board and, using a meat mallet (or the base of a heavy saucepan), lightly bash them, until they are about 1.5cm thick.

Sprinkle lightly with salt and pepper, then, one by one, coat the breasts in the flour and shake off any excess. Dredge them one by one in the egg mixture, then coat in the breadcrumb mixture.

Put the sunflower oil in a saute pan on a medium-high heat.

Once hot, fry one chicken schnitzel for about 2 minutes on each side, until golden, then transfer to a rack set on an oven tray (the rack ensures the bottom of the schnitzels won't go soggy in the oven).

Repeat with the remaining chicken, one breast at a time, then bake in the preheated oven for 7 minutes, or until cooked through.

Cut each schnitzel widthways into 2cm wide strips, then use the knife to transfer each breast neatly to a large platter. Scatter the shallots on top, drizzle over half the dressing and serve with the rest alongside.

CHICKEN THIGH KATSU CURRY

PREPARATION TIME: 15 MINUTES, PLUS 2 HOURS MARINATING | COOKING TIME: 50-60 MINUTES | SERVES 8

My family was missing certain takeaway items during the lockdown due to Covid-19, so I whipped up a few to help their cravings!

INGREDIENTS

FOR THE SAUCE

50ml olive oil

1 brown onion

2 cloves of garlic

1 tsp freshly grated or ground ginger

1 tsp garam masala

1 tbsp medium curry powder

1 medium carrot

150ml vegetable stock

1 tin of coconut milk

1 tbsp maple syrup

Fresh coriander, to garnish

FOR THE CHICKEN

2 heaped tbsp curry powder

500ml milk

8 chicken thighs (bone in)

150g panko breadcrumbs

Salt and pepper, to taste

1½ litres vegetable oil

METHOD

FOR THE SAUCE

Peel and dice the onion, finely chop the garlic, dice the carrot and have the other ingredients to hand. Pour the olive oil into a saucepan on a medium-high heat. Add the onion to the pan and cook for 3 to 5 minutes until tender. Stir in the garlic, ginger, garam masala and curry powder. Mix well and cook for another 2 minutes, then turn the heat down to medium-low.

Add a dash more oil to the pan, add the diced carrot, mix through and cook for 15 minutes, stirring occasionally, until the vegetables are starting to caramelise, but be careful they don't burn.

Pour in the vegetable stock and cook for another 15 minutes, then add the coconut milk and maple syrup. Cook for a final 5 minutes, then remove the pan from the heat.

Blitz up the sauce with a stick blender or in a food processor. You're looking for a thick, smooth consistency. If it gets too thick, add a dash more coconut milk or stock. Season to taste with salt and pepper, adding more maple syrup if needed (but no more than half a tablespoon).

FOR THE CHICKEN

In a large bowl, combine the curry powder thoroughly with the milk, then submerge the chicken thighs in this marinade. Cover with cling film and refrigerate for at least 2 hours.

Remove the marinated chicken from the curried milk, shake off any excess and drop the thighs into the breadcrumbs, then back into the milk, then into the breadcrumbs again, ensuring the chicken is covered completely. You can press the breadcrumbs into the chicken when coating in order to help them stick. Season the coated chicken with salt and pepper.

Pour the vegetable oil into a large pot on a medium-high heat. Heat the oil to 175°c or drop a few breadcrumbs in to see if they turn golden. Carefully lower your coated chicken thighs into the oil (you may need to do this in batches, as the chicken shouldn't be crowded in the pan) and deep fry for 8 to 10 minutes, or until golden brown all over.

Carefully remove the chicken from the oil, drain on a piece of kitchen roll, then serve with the katsu curry sauce garnished with fresh coriander, your choice of rice, maybe a flatbread and definitely a beer!

WILD GARLIC GNOCCHI WITH CHIVE BUTTER

PREPARATION TIME: 25 MINUTES | COOKING TIME: APPROX. 1 HOUR 5 MINUTES | SERVES 2

Cooking brings people together; sitting down around the dinner table each night can be an important time to connect for any household, so making a special yet simple meal like this gnocchi is a wonderful way to celebrate that occasion.

INGREDIENTS

500g floury potatoes

1 egg yolk

50g parmesan, grated

125g tipo 00 flour

Salt and pepper

150g wild garlic leaves (or basil, if out of season)

50g butter, plus extra for cooking the wild garlic

2 or 3 chives

1 head of chive blossom

METHOD

Wash and scrub the potatoes then bake them in the oven at 200-220°c for 45 to 50 minutes or until the potatoes feel soft.

Remove from the oven and allow to cool slightly before scooping out the insides and mashing them with a fork or a potato ricer.

Add the egg yolk and grated parmesan to the mashed potato, mixing everything in while adding the flour bit by bit until it starts to come together. Season with salt and pepper then gently knead the potato mixture on a flat surface until a dough is formed. Cover and set aside until needed.

Wash and dry the wild garlic then roughly chop most of it, reserving a few whole leaves. Heat a large frying pan and wilt the chopped wild garlic in a little butter.

Cut the 50g of butter into small cubes and keep refrigerated. Finely chop the chive stems and pick the blossoms to use later.

On a floured surface, roll the potato dough into sausages of a consistent thickness then slice these into short even pieces.

Roll each piece in your hand to form a small oval shape.

Bring a pan of salted water to the boil, then gently drop in the gnocchi to cook.

They are ready when they rise to the surface of the water, so remove them with a slotted spoon at this point and drain on a clean tea towel. Reserve the cooking water to use later.

Next, dry fry the gnocchi in a heated non-stick pan until browning on both sides. Add the cubes of cold butter, the chopped chives, the whole wild garlic leaves and a generous spoonful of the cooking water to the pan.

Toss everything together to emulsify the butter sauce, then season to taste and garnish with some extra parmesan and the chive blossoms just before serving.

I have known someone who has taken their own life, which really highlighted to me how raising awareness about mental health can help people understand the struggle that others might be going through. Cooking for yourself or others is a small act of kindness that goes a long way. There is something very comforting about the ritual of having a meal around a table, a way to connect with friends and family over food; it's like nourishment for the soul.

ALEX JORGE (@ALEX_JORGE_CHEF)

WILD GARLIC CHICKEN KIEV

PREPARATION TIME: 15 MINUTES, PLUS AT LEAST 2 HOURS CHILLING | COOKING TIME: 12 MINUTES | SERVES 2

Wild garlic has a long season in the UK, from late winter to early spring, and has a milder flavour than bulbs of shop-bought garlic. If you can't find it nearby, spinach works just as well for this comforting dinner.

INGREDIENTS

1 clove of garlic, peeled

100g wild garlic (or spinach, if out of season)

100g butter

2 chicken breasts

50g flour

2 eggs, beaten

50g breadcrumbs

Vegetable oil, for frying

METHOD

Blend the clove of garlic and the wild garlic with the butter until smooth in a food processor, then chill in the fridge for about 30 minutes.

Remove the skin from the chicken breasts then place them between two pieces of cling film and roll or gently tap until flat using a rolling pin.

Remove the cling film and place the garlic butter in the middle of the flattened chicken breasts, dividing it evenly between the two.

Roll the chicken breasts around the filling to enclose it, like a sausage roll, then chill in the fridge until the butter has hardened.

Dip the chicken kievs in the flour, then the beaten egg and finally the breadcrumbs, then chill for at least 1 hour. Overnight is best to completely set the filling and coating.

Cook the kievs by frying them in hot oil for 6 minutes until golden, then transfer to a baking tray and place in a preheated oven at 180°c for another 6 minutes until cooked through.

Allow the chicken kievs to rest for a few minutes before slicing and serving with your choice of greens and sides.

Because I cook as a profession I use other means of release to look after my mental health, like sport. I like to play golf; I find it's a great release for me. My advice on looking after your mental health would be don't take everything to heart. Some things are more important in life and it's good to have perspective on that.

TOM CENCI (@TOMCENCI)

TIM ANDERSON

GARLICKY MUSHROOM & BAMBOO SHOOT GYOZA

PREPARATION TIME: 1 HOUR | COOKING TIME: APPROX. 30 MINUTES | MAKES ABOUT 20

Gyoza are always a joy, even if you don't make them yourself. It's a good idea to keep some in the freezer so you can have them at a moment's notice. Sometimes all you need is a little dumpling fix.

INGREDIENTS

250g mushrooms, finely chopped (just about any kind will do, but I like oyster)

120g bamboo shoots, finely chopped (use a Japanese brand if you can)

15g ginger, peeled and minced

1 tbsp sesame oil

1 tbsp nutritional yeast

Pinch of white pepper

2 tbsp vegetable oil

8 cloves of garlic, minced

1 tbsp flour

½ tsp brown sugar

Salt, to taste

About 20 gyoza wrappers

METHOD

To make the filling, combine the mushrooms, bamboo shoots, ginger, sesame oil, yeast and white pepper in a bowl and mix well. Heat the vegetable oil in a frying pan over a medium heat, add the garlic and saute until barely golden brown, then add the mushroom mixture and continue to cook, stirring often, until the mushrooms have cooked down to about a third of their original size.

Stir in the flour and brown sugar, taste, and add salt as needed.

Lay out a few gyoza wrappers on your counter. Dampen the edge of each wrapper with water using your fingertips. Spoon a generous tablespoon of the filling into the centre then fold the wrapper over the filling and seal. There are two ways I'd advise doing this:

THE NOT TRADITIONAL BUT TOTALLY EASY WAY THAT STILL MAKES VERY CUTE GYOZA

Pinch the wrappers shut to make little half-moon shapes; no need to crimp or pleat but make sure you seal them very tightly. Then, simply curl the ends around to meet each other and pinch them together so you end up with shapes like tortelloni.

THE TRADITIONAL AND SOMEWHAT MORE DIFFICULT WAY THAT WILL IMPRESS YOUR JAPANESE MOTHER-IN-LAW

Fold the wrappers over the filling but don't seal them. Instead, pinch the wrapper shut at one end. Then, use the index finger of your dominant hand to keep the filling 'tucked in' as you crimp and pinch the wrapper to seal it; use your thumb to pleat the side of the wrapper closest to you, and with each pleat, pinch it firmly onto the opposite side of the wrapper. You should get about five pleats into each gyoza before you reach the other end, then simply pinch that corner shut to finish it off.

These will result in lovely, traditionally crescent-shaped gyoza.

Place the gyoza sealed side up on a lined or cornflour-dusted tray, keeping them covered with a damp cloth as you work. At this point, you can keep them wrapped in cling film in the fridge for a day, or freeze them on the tray until solid then transfer to an airtight container until needed.

To cook the gyoza, heat about a tablespoon of oil in a non-stick pan with a well-fitting lid over a high heat. Add as many gyoza as will fit, and when they are sizzling, pour in about 100ml of water and place the lid on the pan. Steam for 5 minutes, then remove the lid and let all the water evaporate. The gyoza should have nice crispy golden-brown bottoms but if they're still quite pale when the water is gone, just keep cooking them for another couple of minutes.

Tip the gyoza out onto a plate, and serve with 'gyoza sauce' which is three parts soy sauce to one part vinegar, with a few drops of chilli oil or sesame oil, for dipping.

JERK CHICKEN

PREPARATION TIME: 10 MINUTES, PLUS 6-12 HOURS MARINATING | COOKING TIME: 20 MINUTES | SERVES 6

I produced this recipe when I was a chef trainer at the University of West London. The students and customers loved it.

INGREDIENTS

1 scotch bonnet, cored and roughly chopped

3 spring onions, chopped

80g root ginger, peeled and chopped

2 cloves of garlic, crushed

20g tomato paste

3 sprigs of thyme, leaves picked and stalks discarded)

2 tbsp dried parsley

1 tbsp ground cinnamon

1 tbsp ground allspice

1½ tbsp smoked paprika

½ tbsp cayenne pepper

½ tbsp white pepper

4 tsp sea salt

150g muscovado sugar

150g Canadian maple syrup

1 tbsp rapeseed oil

2kg chicken wings (ask your butcher to remove the tips)

330ml premium lager (San Miguel or Red Stripe works great)

3 limes, zested and juiced

2 limes, cut into wedges

Fresh coriander leaves

METHOD

Using a food processor, blitz the scary hot scotch bonnet, spring onions, ginger, garlic, tomato paste, thyme, parsley, spices, salt, sugar, maple syrup and oil together until a loose paste forms.

Find a large tray big enough to fit all the chicken wings in, or several suitable containers. If you have food safe gloves, get those bad boys on. If not, wash your hands before you go to the toilet, or you're in a world of pain.

Smother all the wings in the paste. Do not be shy and ensure every part of every wing is covered. Cover the chicken and refrigerate for 6 to 12 hours. Ideally, prepare this the day before and marinate overnight.

When you're ready to cook, preheat the oven to 160°c and prepare a skillet. Alternatively, get the barbecue roaring.

Line a baking tray with a baking sheet or greaseproof paper. Take the wings out of the marinade, keeping everything left in the containers, and place them on the lined baking tray. Bake the wings for 15 minutes in the preheated oven.

In the meantime, put all the remaining marinade into a saucepan. Do not waste a drop; this is flavour town. Add the beer and all the lime zest and juice with a splash of water. Bring to the boil then turn down to a simmer.

Cook until the amount has reduced by half to create a glaze.

Once your skillet or barbecue is roaring hot (nearly smoking) remove your wings from the oven and get them cooking. You should hear a very intense sizzle.

Cook the wings for 1 to 2 minutes on each side until they turn a deep dark charred colour, then apply the thick jerk glaze to each wing. Serve with the lime wedges and fresh coriander leaves.

I'm always keen to push the ever-growing mental health awareness cause because it means a lot to me on a personal level. Cooking provides a platform to be artistic and creative, to bring happiness and joy to not only yourself but to those you are cooking for, no matter what you are making. Self-belief and self-care are everything. No one is more important than yourself.

JACK BLUMENTHAL (@JACK_BLUMENTHAL)

KING PRAWN & PEA RISOTTO

PREPARATION TIME: 5 MINUTES | COOKING TIME: APPROX. 45 MINUTES | SERVES 4-6

Kitchens are very intense places to cook and work, but ironically I find cooking relaxes me! Stirring risotto can be a calming activity, and the more you stir the better the texture will be.

INGREDIENTS

2 shallots or 1 small onion

Sprig of thyme

3 cloves of garlic

100ml extra-virgin olive oil

500g risotto rice

Glug of white wine

1 litre water

Fish or chicken stock cubes

300g raw king prawns, defrosted if frozen

75g frozen peas

50g mascarpone or creme fraiche

Parmesan, grated (optional)

Fresh dill, tarragon or parsley

METHOD

Finely dice the shallot or onion, chop the thyme and crush the cloves of garlic.

Sweat the prepared onions, thyme and garlic in the olive oil (reserving a little for later) until soft.

Next, add the rice and fry for 5 to 6 minutes, stirring to coat the grains in the oil.

Add the white wine and cook on a moderate heat, stirring constantly, until the wine has been absorbed by the rice. Boil the litre of water then dissolve the stock cubes in it.

Slowly add the stock to the rice little by little, and keep stirring constantly until the rice is cooked but not mushy. This should take around 20 minutes.

Add the prawns and the peas to the risotto then cook for 4 more minutes until the prawns are pink and the peas tender.

Remove the pan from the heat and fold in the mascarpone or creme fraiche. If you like, add some grated parmesan to taste at this stage.

Finish the risotto with some finely chopped herbs of your choice, then divide between flat plates and drizzle with a little olive oil just before serving.

Mental health is a big issue, especially in my industry, so anything we can do to raise awareness is a good thing. To look after my own mental health, I talk to my friends and family and am honest when I feel things are not great or stressful. Talk more and don't bottle up your emotions; it's OK to be 'weak' sometimes.

ASHLEY CLARKE (@CHEF_CLARKE)

LAMB SHAPTA

PREPARATION TIME: 15 MINUTES | COOKING TIME: 20-25 MINUTES | SERVES 4

This is one of my favourite recipes and something I like to cook often. The inspiration came from Northeast India and Tibet, where shapta is usually made with beef or yak meat, but this version involves deep fried lamb.

INGREDIENTS

400g lamb fillet
2 tbsp oil, plus extra for deep frying
2 tbsp finely chopped garlic
4 whole red chillies, split open
2 red and yellow peppers, cut into strips
1 medium pak choi, cut into strips
Spring onion greens, cut into strips
Knob of ginger, cut into strips

FOR THE SHAPTA SAUCE

2 tbsp finely chopped garlic
1 tbsp red chilli flakes and seeds
100ml light soy sauce
¼ tsp timur or Szechuan pepper powder
¼ tsp ground black pepper
1 tsp sugar
200ml light tomato sauce or ketchup

FOR THE MARINADE

1 tbsp cornflour
1 tbsp rice wine
1 egg
Pinch of salt
Pinch of Szechuan pepper

METHOD

First, make the shapta sauce.

Heat a little oil in a frying pan then saute the garlic and chilli flakes. Add the soy sauce, timur or Szechuan pepper powder, black pepper, sugar and tomato sauce or ketchup. Stir in two tablespoons of water and simmer for a few minutes, then take the pan off the heat.

Combine all the ingredients for the marinade in a shallow bowl.

Slice the lamb fillet thinly and coat the meat in the marinade. Heat a pan one third full of oil and deep fry the lamb slices until crisp and light brown in colour. Transfer the lamb to a tray lined with kitchen paper so the excess oil is absorbed.

Heat the remaining two tablespoons of oil in a wok, then saute the garlic and whole red chillies.

Add the fried lamb and peppers, cook for 1 to 2 minutes and then add the shapta sauce. Add the pak choi and spring onion greens, saute for 2 to 3 minutes and then add the ginger.

Stir briefly to combine everything and serve hot.

Having gone through personal tough times, I know how important it is to have a balanced mind, body and soul. Looking after my fellow industry men and women is more important than ever, as we all suffer from mental trauma and illness from time to time. It needs healing as much as any physical illness, except these scars are much deeper and more painful. Since cooking is a passion, it takes my mind away from uncertainties. I find myself to be a lot happier and more focused in the kitchen.

ATUL KOCHHAR (@CHEFATULKOCHHAR)

SAFFRON CHICKEN

PREPARATION TIME: 20 MINUTES | COOKING TIME: 40-50 MINUTES | SERVES 8

The journey of this recipe started when I decided to recreate my dad's family classic that would also suit a tasting menu. The secret is quality chicken stock and saffron; I always do homemade stock and use Iranian saffron. Enjoy!

INGREDIENTS

1kg desiree potatoes

Olive oil

4 onions

1 cinnamon stick

3 cloves of garlic

2 generous pinches of saffron

1 tbsp ground fennel

1 tsp ground cumin

1 tsp ground coriander

600ml good quality chicken stock

8 chicken breasts (boneless thighs are a good alternative)

Salt and pepper

1 litre sunflower oil, for deep frying

Handful of golden sultanas

Generous squeeze of honey (optional)

½ a lemon, juiced

Red amaranth micro herbs, to garnish

METHOD

Begin by peeling the potatoes and rinsing them under cold water.

Cube the potatoes and cook in salted boiling water until al dente. Drain and place into cold water when done.

To make the saffron sauce, finely dice one of the onions. Add a glug of olive oil to a saucepan and sweat the onion with the cinnamon stick. After 5 minutes, grate two of the garlic cloves and add them to the pan, increasing the heat slightly. Fry for 2 minutes.

Meanwhile, bruise the saffron in a pestle and mortar with a splash of water. This allows the saffron to 'bleed' which releases a more intense flavour. Add the bruised saffron and the ground spices to the pan, fry for another 2 minutes, then add the chicken stock. Turn the heat down low and let those ingredients infuse for the next 30 minutes, stirring occasionally. You should see the saffron strands begin to turn the sauce a rich yellow colour and the smells should be delightful.

Meanwhile, season the chicken, using only salt on the skin side. Place a frying pan with a little oil on a medium heat and sear the chicken skin side down, without turning over. You are looking for a crisp skin and golden colour which should take no more than 6 to 8 minutes. Once golden, transfer to a baking tray, flesh side down. Preheat the oven to 180°c fan.

Pour the sunflower oil into a large pot on a medium heat. Cut the remaining onions in half and slice them as thinly as possible. Once the oil has heated, fry the onions until brown. Transfer to a plate lined with kitchen paper to drain and season with salt.

At this point, place the chicken in the preheated oven for 15 minutes. Meanwhile, taste the saffron sauce for seasoning and add the golden sultanas, a squeeze of honey and the lemon juice. Add more according to your preference for sweet or sour flavour. Check if the juices run clear in the chicken, cooking for longer if they are pink. When done, leave to rest for 5 minutes.

To serve, spoon the sauce generously over the potatoes. Place a piece of chicken on top of the potatoes, top with the crispy onions and dress the border of the plate with red amaranth. Enjoy!

I have really benefited from working on myself over the past five years. I've discovered so many aspects of myself that were hidden from my view, but were impacting me and people around me. One thing that stands out was my inability to share and be more vulnerable with people in my life. I'd often get stopped by what people would think and if that would be seen as acceptable. I've come to realise that our minds can often be a big trap. Self-expression is missing in so many of us and that is where the magic is!

PHILIP JUMA (@JUMAKITCHEN)

CARI LAMB CURRY

PREPARATION TIME: 15 MINUTES | COOKING TIME: APPROX. 3 HOURS | SERVES 4-6

Lamb is a wonderfully rich meat that can handle lots of chilli and spice. I cooked this dish in the MasterChef final and still can't believe that one of my family's classic curries was enough to secure me the title!

INGREDIENTS

3 tbsp vegetable oil

1 onion, finely chopped

5 cloves of garlic, finely chopped

2.5cm piece of ginger, peeled and finely grated

3 red bird's eye chillies, finely chopped (with seeds)

Handful of curry leaves (around 10-12)

3 tbsp finely chopped coriander stalks

3 tbsp madras curry powder

1 tsp ground cumin

1 tsp ground coriander

½ tsp fenugreek seeds

1 stick of cinnamon, snapped into pieces

500g lamb shoulder, chopped into 2.5cm cubes

1 x 400g tin of plum tomatoes

300ml water

Salt and white pepper

3 tbsp finely chopped coriander leaves

METHOD

Heat the oil in a large pan over a medium heat and gently fry the onion, garlic, ginger and chilli until softened slightly.

Add the curry leaves, coriander stalks, ground spices, fenugreek seeds and cinnamon with a splash of water. Cook for about 1 minute until fragrant.

Add the lamb to brown it evenly on all sides, which should take around 15 minutes. Add the tinned tomatoes and water then reduce to a simmer.

Cover with a lid and cook for 2 and a half to 3 hours, stirring occasionally. When the curry is cooked, the lamb should be tender and the sauce thickened to a gravy consistency.

Season the curry with salt and white pepper, taste and adjust accordingly. Stir in the fresh coriander leaves. You can also add fried onions at this point as a garnish.

Serve with warm roti, fresh salad and some mango pickle. It tastes even better the next day as all the spices harmonise and the flavours go deep into the meat.

Whenever I have a low day I just take myself into the kitchen, put on some music and immerse myself in my spices and cook books and play around with whatever I can find. I almost always instantly feel better. It's like hitting reset.
SHELINA PERMALLOO (@SHELINACOOKS)

SLOW COOKED SHORT RIB LASAGNE

PREPARATION TIME: 30 MINUTES | COOKING TIME: AT LEAST 6 HOURS | SERVES 8

This is a bit of a labour of love, but trust me, it's worth it! The short ribs are cooked in the tomato sauce until they fall apart, giving you an incredibly rich ragu to build the lasagne with.

INGREDIENTS

FOR THE RAGU

2 tbsp olive oil

800g short ribs

Knob of butter

2 shallots, finely sliced

2 sticks of celery, finely diced

2 medium carrots, finely diced

3 cloves of garlic, crushed

100ml marsala or sherry (optional)

300ml red wine

2 bay leaves

A few sprigs of rosemary

100ml whole milk

2 tins of peeled plum tomatoes

FOR THE BECHAMEL

80g butter

80g plain flour

800ml whole milk

Salt and pepper

Pinch of grated nutmeg

2 tbsp grated parmesan

TO ASSEMBLE

Around 20 dried lasagne sheets

50g grated parmesan or pecorino

METHOD

FOR THE RAGU

You'll need the best part of the day to make this so start early if you're planning on eating in the evening. Add the olive oil to a very large, ovenproof, heavy-bottomed pan that will fit all of the ribs in and has a lid. Over a medium heat, fry the short ribs in batches until browned on all sides. Set aside then clean any burnt bits out of the pan with some kitchen roll. Preheat the oven to 130°c.

Melt the butter in the same large pan over a medium heat until sizzling. Add the shallots, celery, carrot and garlic then cook gently until soft but not coloured. Turn the heat up slightly and add the marsala, if using, then bring to the boil. Add the wine and cook out for around 5 minutes, until the sharpness has come out of the alcohol.

Put the short ribs back into the pan with the bay and rosemary. Add the milk, then squeeze the plum tomatoes into the pan to crush them. Season with salt and pepper then bring to the boil. Put the lid on and place in the preheated oven for at least 5 hours, until the meat is incredibly soft and flakes away easily from the bones. Leave the ragu to cool slightly, then remove the bones, bay leaves and rosemary from the sauce. Shred the meat with two forks, removing any remaining sinew.

FOR THE BECHAMEL

Melt the butter in a medium pan, and then whisk in the flour. Cook for a couple of minutes, stirring constantly, then gradually whisk in the milk, and bring to the boil, still stirring. Season with the salt, pepper, nutmeg and parmesan then simmer for about 5 minutes until thickened.

When you're ready to assemble your lasagne, preheat the oven to 200°c. Fill a large baking tray with just-boiled water and place the lasagne sheets in it to soften slightly.

Take a deep, wide dish and coat the bottom with a third of the ragu, topped with a quarter of the bechamel, then a layer of lasagne sheets. Repeat to make two more layers, and then top the last layer of pasta with the rest of the bechamel and the grated parmesan or pecorino.

Bake the lasagne for 40 minutes in the preheated oven until golden and bubbling.

Try to care less about what people think of you, and surround yourself with people that celebrate you rather than those that try to undermine you and make you smaller. I struggled with anxiety for a while when I was a teenager but I didn't know what it was then. I would have really appreciated someone telling me that it was normal! These days, my job is quite stressful and I like to wind down by cooking. You can always trust that putting together ingredients in a certain way will create something delicious and that's very comforting to me.

GIOVANNA RYAN (@GIOVANNARYAN)

CHICKEN, CHORIZO & RIOJA SPANISH-STYLE STEW

PREPARATION TIME: 5 MINUTES | COOKING TIME: 2 HOURS 30 MINUTES | SERVES 6-8

This is a really comforting recipe that I prepare with love on a regular basis for my family.
It's one of our favourites that I hope will become a firm favourite with you too!

INGREDIENTS

2 tbsp olive oil

8 chicken thighs

80g cooking chorizo

2 red bell peppers

2 red onions

2 white onions

4 cloves of garlic

1 small red chilli

500ml chicken stock

250ml Rioja (any other red wine is fine, but less authentically Spanish)

2 sprigs of fresh thyme

1 tsp paprika

Salt and pepper

50g fresh spinach

METHOD

Preheat the oven to 180°c fan.

Heat the olive oil in a large ovenproof pot or casserole with a lid on the stove.

Fry the chicken thighs in the hot oil so that they brown slightly, then remove them from the pot. Slice the chorizo into fairly large pieces (about half a centimetre thick) and fry in the pot for 2 minutes until browned and crispy on the outside. Remove from the pot.

Slice the peppers and onions, then add them to the pot to cook in the olive oil and the oil released from the chorizo.

Cook for about 5 minutes until softened and translucent. Meanwhile, slice or crush the garlic and thinly slice the chilli. Add these to the pot and cook for another couple of minutes.

Put the chicken thighs and chorizo back into the pot, then pour over the stock and red wine. Pick the leaves from the thyme sprigs and sprinkle them into the stew. Add the paprika and season everything well with salt and pepper.

Turn up the heat until the liquid is bubbling, then put the lid on the pot and transfer it to the preheated oven. Cook for about 2 hours until the chicken thighs and vegetables are tender and the sauce has reduced by half.

Lay the fresh spinach in a large serving dish then spoon over the stew and all the juices.

Place the dish in the oven for 5 minutes to wilt the spinach, then take it to the table and serve.

Cooking definitely calms me down. It's my happy place and my escape from the stresses of the outside world. It allows me to focus on the task in hand and create something with love for the people I care about. I suffer with anxiety, so I'm always happy to help out a charity that educates people on mental illnesses. There needs to be less stigma attached to asking for help. Talk to someone; don't suffer in silence. You're not alone and you're not strange for having the feelings that you do.

EMMA OXLEY (@EMMAEATSANDEXPLORES)

NEVER BE AFRAID TO TALK TO PEOPLE ABOUT THE THINGS YOU MAY FEEL ASHAMED OR AFRAID OF.

PEOPLE ARE NOT JUDGING YOU AS MUCH AS YOU THINK THEY ARE, AND EVEN IF THEY ARE – WHO CARES?

TIM ANDERSON (@CHEFTIMANDERSON)

LANCASHIRE HOTPOT

PREPARATION TIME: 20-30 MINUTES | COOKING TIME: 2 HOURS 10-20 MINUTES | SERVES 2

Something magical happens to these few simple ingredients when cooked slowly together; the resulting hotpot really is so comforting and delicious.

INGREDIENTS

50g plain flour

Salt and pepper

1 tsp caster sugar

2 Barnsley chops or 4 lamb cutlets

2 large baking potatoes

1 large onion

3 sprigs of thyme

300ml good quality stock (if not lamb, chicken or even vegetable will do)

15g butter, melted

METHOD

First put the flour, salt, pepper and sugar in a bowl or bag, add the meat and stir or shake to coat the lamb.

Preheat the oven to 160°c fan while you peel and thinly slice the potatoes (use a mandoline if you have one; I don't always bother to peel the potatoes but do this first if you prefer) and the onion.

I like to use either a small lidded cast-iron pot or a loaf tin to make this dish.

Cover the bottom of the pot or tin with a layer of overlapping potato slices. Add plenty of salt and pepper.

Lay the lamb chops, not overlapping each other, over the potatoes, lay the thyme on top and then lay the onion slices on top of that.

Season the onions, then layer the remaining potato slices on top, overlapping them as neatly as you can.

Pour the stock carefully into the pot or tin, enough to come up to but not cover the top layer of potatoes.

Brush the top layer of potatoes with the melted butter and add a little more salt and pepper. Cover with a lid or a tight layer of tin foil and bake for about 2 hours in the preheated oven.

Carefully uncover and put back into the oven until the potato on top is burnished and crunchy. Serve from the pot.

Good food is an important part of good mental health, and sharing makes us stronger, whether that's a recipe for comfort food or a story of vulnerability. This dish, for me, represents the importance of treasuring simple things; lamb cutlets were the first food I craved after finishing chemotherapy. I also like to take walks with my dog, play backgammon with my husband and focus on my breath when things feel overwhelming.

LISA MARKWELL (@HOLDSKNIFELIKEPEN)

COTTAGE PIE

PREPARATION TIME: 25-30 MINUTES | COOKING TIME: I HOUR 10 MINUTES | SERVES 6

Me and my partner have cooked this the same way for 12 years and it's never changed. It's not the fanciest recipe, but it works so well when you're cooking at home and don't have stocks to hand for the gravy.

INGREDIENTS

1.2kg Maris Piper potatoes
Pinch of salt
I onion
750g beef mince (5% fat)
300ml boiling water
2 beef stock cubes
2 tbsp Bisto gravy granules
4 tbsp brown sauce
160g raw or tinned carrots, sliced
200g frozen peas
Knob of butter
Splash of milk

METHOD

Start by peeling the potatoes and cutting them into equally sized pieces.

Place the potatoes in a large pan with enough water to cover them, season well with salt and place the pan on a high heat. Bring to the boil, then turn down to a medium heat and cook until tender.

While the potatoes are cooking, dice the onion and saute in a large saucepan with a little oil. When the onion is starting to caramelise, remove it from the pan and add the beef mince. Start on a low to medium heat, and once the meat starts to change colour, add the boiling water.

After 5 minutes, add the stock cubes and stir well for a further 3 minutes, then add the gravy granules, stirring well the whole time. Once you add the granules, the mixture will begin to thicken so use a little more water to loosen the sauce if needed.

To finish, add the brown sauce to taste. I love to add lots as it gives the mince a sweet and sour flavour which goes really well with the mash. Set the pan aside off the heat.

Boil a small pan of water and add the sliced carrots if you're using raw ones, along with the frozen peas. Cook until tender, then drain and stir the vegetables into the mince and gravy.

By now the potatoes should be ready to mash, so drain off the water and place the potatoes back in the pan. Add two large spoonfuls of butter and some milk. I love using salted butter here. Mash the potatoes until smooth.

Place the filling into an ovenproof dish (such as a Pyrex) leaving space for the mash, which can be spread over the top with a fork. Once you have an even layer, drag the fork over the mash to ruffle it up; this will help it turn nice and crispy in the oven. If you want to take it to the next level, you can pipe the mash over the filling with a nozzle fitted into a plastic bag.

Bake the cottage pie for 30 to 40 minutes in a preheated oven at 175°c until bubbling and golden brown, then serve up.

When I go to work, it gives me the chance to think about nothing else but food, and when I cook at home, it gives me a chance to reflect and unwind. I try to exercise four or five times a week too; this is when I switch off, listen to music and concentrate on the running. My main advice for looking after your mental health would be never bottle anything up, always tell someone how you're feeling.

ELLIOT PLIMMER (@CHEF_ELLIOT)

CHICKEN PIE

PREPARATION TIME: 15 MINUTES | COOKING TIME: 25-35 MINUTES | SERVES 2

A healthy twist on a familiar favourite. Chicken is rich in protein, zinc and B vitamins, while sweet potatoes are a great source of fibre and beta-carotene. If you prefer white ones, leave the skin on to retain the fibre.

INGREDIENTS

500g white or sweet potatoes

5 tbsp olive oil

300g skinless and boneless chicken thighs or breasts, chopped into 2cm chunks

1 leek, sliced

10 brown mushrooms, diced

1 lemon, zested and juiced

2 tbsp wholegrain flour

50ml water

3 tbsp creme fraiche

½-1 tsp wholegrain mustard, to taste

METHOD

Preheat the oven to 180°c fan.

If you're using white potatoes, leave the skins on and chop them into small chunks. Boil them in a pan of salted water until they are soft. The cooking time will depend on the size of the chunks but it should take no more than 15 to 20 minutes.

If you're using sweet potatoes, peel them and chop them into chunks, toss them in one tablespoon of the olive oil then bake them in the preheated oven for 15 to 20 minutes, or until they are soft (sweet potatoes absorb too much water if they are boiled).

While the potatoes cook, heat a pan and fry the chicken with the leek in two tablespoons of the olive oil for 3 minutes, then add the mushrooms and lemon zest and cook for another 3 to 5 minutes. The chicken pieces should be around 80 percent cooked by this point.

Add the flour to thicken the mixture, stirring for around 2 minutes. Add the water and stir in half the juice from the lemon, the creme fraiche and mustard, then take the pan off the heat.

Once the potatoes are cooked, mash them with the remaining olive oil.

Spoon the chicken filling into a small baking dish, or two individual ramekins, and spread the mashed potato over the top.

Bake the pie(s) for 10 to 15 minutes in the oven and if you wish, you can place them under the grill to brown the mash before serving.

*Recipe © Rachel Kelly from The Happy Kitchen: Good Mood Food by Rachel Kelly and Alice Mackintosh

My advice to my younger self would be that it is not selfish to look after your mental health. It allows you to help others in turn. Eating with your mental health in mind is a great place to start looking after yourself. I believe food can influence our mood, and this recipe came about because of my collaboration with the nutritional therapist Alice Mackintosh. The resulting dishes are all based on scientific research about what ingredients help with low mood. Food is at the heart of the strategies I use to look after my mental health, along with mindfulness, healing poetry and exercise.

RACHEL KELLY (@RACHELFKELLY)

LIA TEIXEIRA

MEAT CROQUETTES WITH ROSE HARISSA MAYONNAISE

PREPARATION TIME: 1 HOUR 30 MINUTES | COOKING TIME: APPROX. 1 HOUR | MAKES 20 TO 24

I'm Portuguese and this recipe is a very special family favourite. My mum is a great cook and she's a master at making pastries. Meat croquettes are one of her specialties and she taught me how to make these.

INGREDIENTS

500g leftover cooked meat

25g butter

1 tbsp olive oil

1 medium onion, finely chopped

3 cloves of garlic, crushed

50g plain flour, plus extra for coating

250ml whole milk, boiled

2 tbsp finely chopped fresh parsley

Pinch of grated nutmeg

Sea salt and ground black pepper

2 large eggs, beaten

Breadcrumbs, to coat

1 litre vegetable oil, for deep frying

Mayonnaise, for dipping

Rose harissa paste

METHOD

First, mince your leftover cooked meat in a food processor.

Meanwhile, heat the butter and olive oil in a large pan over a medium-high heat.

Add the onion and garlic then cook while stirring for 3 minutes or until the onion is soft and golden brown.

Sprinkle in the flour and stir continuously until a paste forms; this is called a roux. Continue cooking for 2 minutes. Add the hot milk to the roux gradually, stirring as you go, until you get a smooth sauce.

Cook for 5 to 10 minutes, stirring continuously, until the sauce has thickened.

Take the pan off the heat and add the meat, chopped parsley, nutmeg, sea salt and freshly ground black pepper to taste. Transfer the mixture to a bowl and allow to cool.

Divide the mixture into 20 to 24 pieces, all approximately the same weight so they cook evenly. Dust your hands well with flour and shape the croquettes into sausages or, if you prefer, golf balls.

Put some flour into a shallow bowl and roll each croquette in it to coat them.

Next, dip the croquettes in the beaten egg, followed by the breadcrumbs.

Place your coated croquettes in a large baking tray, cover with cling film and refrigerate for 1 hour or until firm.

Heat the vegetable oil in a large cast iron pan until it reaches 180°c (you can also do this in a deep-fat fryer). If you can't measure the temperature, a piece of bread should sizzle and turn golden in 15 to 20 seconds when the oil is hot enough.

Deep fry three or four croquettes at a time in the oil, lifting them out once golden brown using a slotted spoon.

Leave to drain on a plate lined with kitchen paper until all the croquettes are fried.

Serve the croquettes with a bowl of mayonnaise swirled with rose harissa paste for dipping, or, if you prefer, a bowl of Dijon mustard.

When I moved to the UK in 2007, my English was very poor and I had no friends or family here (apart from my husband and six year old son, whom I moved with). My husband was working all day, five days a week and apart from dropping off and picking up my son at school and shopping, my life was very lonely, especially that first year. Watching cooking programmes on TV and then cooking and replicating the recipes by myself helped me greatly, not just by keeping me sane and mentally busy, but also improving my English.

LIA TEIXEIRA (@LIALEMONANDVANILLA)

AMY LANZA

BUTTERNUT SQUASH MAC 'N' CHEESE

PREPARATION TIME: 10-15 MINUTES | COOKING TIME: 1 HOUR | SERVES 2

A warming, comforting bowl of the classic with a plant-based and healthier twist. The sauce is thick, creamy, flavoursome and vibrant with added vegetables; a great meal to show off how vibrant, wholesome and delicious vegan food can be.

INGREDIENTS

FOR THE SAUCE

½ a butternut squash (200-250g flesh)

4 tbsp plant-based milk

2 tbsp tahini or olive oil

2 tbsp nutritional yeast

½ tsp each of smoked paprika, ground turmeric and Dijon mustard

FOR THE PASTA

Olive oil

½ a white onion, finely diced

1 small courgette, finely diced

2 cloves of garlic, crushed

1 tbsp tamari

180g pasta of your choice

160g frozen peas

1 handful of spinach, chopped

10 cherry tomatoes, halved

FOR THE 'CHEESY' TOPPING

1 tbsp shelled hemp seeds

1 tbsp nutritional yeast

¼ tsp ground turmeric

METHOD

FOR THE SAUCE

Preheat the oven to 180°c fan and line a tray with baking parchment.

Place the butternut squash cut side up on the tray and drizzle with a bit of olive oil. Roast in the oven for 40 to 50 minutes or until tender and starting to brown at the edges. Remove from the oven and allow to cool.

Scoop out and discard the seeds, then scoop out the flesh and place it in a food processor with the remaining ingredients. Blend until smooth, scraping down the sides as necessary and seasoning to taste.

You may need to add a splash more milk to make a runnier sauce. This can be made up to 2 days in advance when kept cool in an airtight container in the fridge.

FOR THE PASTA

Heat a good drizzle of olive oil in a saucepan and fry the onion for 10 minutes until caramelising and translucent. Now add the courgette and garlic and continue to fry for 5 to 7 minutes until cooked through, adding the tamari for the last minute.

Meanwhile, cook the pasta according to the packet instructions, adding the peas for the final 5 minutes. Drain, reserving some of the cooking water, and leave to one side.

FOR THE 'CHEESY' TOPPING

Make the topping by mixing all the ingredients together in a bowl. Season to taste.

TO SERVE

Return the cooked pasta to the saucepan then add the onion and courgette mixture, chopped spinach, tomatoes, butternut sauce and four tablespoons of the cooking water. Stir the pasta over a low heat until creamy and well coated in sauce, adding more cooking water if required.

Divide the pasta between two bowls and sprinkle over the 'cheesy' hemp topping.

I am passionate about mental health and encouraging conversation so we can all live happier and healthier lives, one step at a time. I try to do small things every day like starting the morning with a cosy hot drink in bed, repeating a few affirmations and switching off from social media at a set time. I try to be as open as possible with my feelings at home and with friends. I practice self-care each day, too, from a comforting latte to unwinding with a bubble bath, going for a walk in the fresh air and enjoying good food.

AMY LANZA (@NOURISHING.AMY)

STRAWBERRY GAZPACHO

PREPARATION TIME: 10 MINUTES, PLUS INFUSING OVERNIGHT | COOKING TIME: 5 MINUTES | SERVES 6

Gazpacho is a lovely super-fresh vegetable soup. It's very popular in Andalusia, southern Spain, where they have really high temperatures during summer and this rich but cold dish is perfect!

INGREDIENTS

700g ripe strawberries, plus a few reserved for garnishing

300g vine-ripened tomatoes, chopped

1 roasted red pepper, sliced

1 small shallot, finely chopped

1 small clove of garlic, crushed

1 tbsp sherry vinegar

75ml extra-virgin olive oil, plus extra for frying and serving

Sea salt and freshly ground black pepper

2 slices of sourdough bread, diced

Basil leaves and edible flowers, to garnish

METHOD

In a large bowl, combine the strawberries, tomatoes, roasted red pepper, shallot, garlic and sherry vinegar. Toss all the ingredients together then leave to infuse overnight.

The next day, add the extra-virgin olive oil to the bowl and whizz everything together with a hand blender or in a food processor until smooth, adding a splash of water if it's too thick. Season the gazpacho to taste with salt and pepper.

Pour a little olive oil into a frying pan over a medium heat and fry the sourdough croutons for 4 to 5 minutes, until golden on all sides. Drain on kitchen paper and sprinkle with sea salt.

Divide the gazpacho between individual soup bowls and garnish with the extra strawberries, basil leaves, edible flowers and sourdough croutons.

Finish with a drizzle of extra-virgin olive oil and some sea salt.

Serve with a cold glass of sherry, preferably amontillado or palo cortado.

*From Andalusia: Recipes from Seville and Beyond, published by Hardie Grant

I wanted to contribute to this lovely cause because cooking is one of the most amazing creative outlets that improves mental health. For me it's like meditation. Since Covid, I've started doing yoga every week to remind me to breathe properly and to stretch the old bones. Work provides structure and purpose but I know this is challenging for many people at the moment. I suggest creating some sort of routine each day and keeping busy so you don't become depressed. Friendships and relationships are the absolute key to good mental health, food and cooking is all about this – bringing people together.

JOSÉ PIZARRO (@JOSE_PIZARRO)

"THOSE FEELGOOD VIBES DON'T JUST HAVE TO COME FROM RUNNING OR SWEATING; YOU CAN GRAB THEM FROM YOUR WAFFLES, COOKIES, BROWNIES, OR SLICE OF CAKE.

CHAPTER FIVE

SWEET TREATS

Welcome to the chapter you've been waiting for!

Why do we love dessert so much? For me, it's the perfect end to an evening out with friends, something to look forward to in the morning for breakfast, or just a midday pick-me-up.

It also doesn't hurt that sweets contain endorphins. Those feelgood vibes don't just have to come from running or sweating; you can grab them from your waffles, cookies, brownies, or slice of cake.

I feel like baking is a form of therapy, whether you do it by yourself or with others. It's also a bonding experience! There's nothing like burning your first batch of cookies with your son, daughter or partner then trying again and again.

I won't keep you here for long; enjoy the recipes and be on the lookout for my Date Night Cookies. Enjoy!

Haya Khalifeh
(@butterbelieveit)

MANGO & PASSION FRUIT PAVLOVAS

PREPARATION TIME: 2 HOURS | COOKING TIME: I HOUR | MAKES 4 (ENOUGH FOR 8-10 PEOPLE SHARING)

All my recipes remind me of moments shared, of gatherings. Pavlovas have been at so many dinners and iftars, and they always bring joy and a certain celebratory mood to dessert.

INGREDIENTS

FOR THE MERINGUE NESTS

4 large egg whites

200g caster sugar

Pinch of cream of tartar

I tsp vanilla extract

A few drops of coconut essence (optional)

Shredded coconut, to sprinkle

FOR THE PASSION FRUIT MASCARPONE CREAM

250g mascarpone

200ml whipping cream

I tsp vanilla extract

A few drops of coconut essence (optional)

4 fresh ripe passion fruits

FOR THE TOPPINGS

Fresh mango, cubed

Pomegranate seeds

Shredded coconut

METHOD

FOR THE MERINGUE NESTS

Preheat the oven to 100°c and line a couple of baking trays with non-stick baking paper.

Place the egg whites, caster sugar and cream of tartar in the bowl of a stand mixer, then make a bain-marie by placing the bowl over a pan with a few centimetres of simmering water in. Whisk the mixture by hand for 2 to 3 minutes until it warms up a bit and the sugar dissolves.

Dry the bottom of the bowl and transfer to the stand mixer. Whisk on high speed until stiff peaks form, then fold in the vanilla and the coconut essence if using.

Place two or three tablespoons of meringue for each nest on the lined trays, spreading in a circular shape to make a well in the middle that will hold the cream.

Sprinkle the meringues with a little shredded coconut, lower the oven temperature to 90°c and place the trays in the oven.

Bake the meringues for about I hour, or until the nests are dry and can be lifted from the tray.

FOR THE PASSION FRUIT MASCARPONE CREAM

Place the mascarpone in a bowl and whisk until creamy. Add the whipping cream and whip on medium-high speed until the mixture is thick and fluffy, but don't over-whip or it could split. Gently fold in the vanilla and the coconut essence if using.

Halve the passion fruits and scoop out the centres, then fold the passion fruit into the cream just before assembling the pavlovas.

When the meringue nests are completely cool, fill them with the passion fruit cream, top with the cubed mango and pomegranate seeds, sprinkle with shredded coconut and serve immediately.

You can keep the cooled meringues, without any fillings or toppings, in an airtight container for up to a week. The cream can be prepared up to a day in advance and the pavlovas should be assembled just before serving.

My advice on looking after your mental health has been the same for quite a while: put your oxygen mask first before helping others. If we are ok, if we are happy and strong, then we can help others. In French, there is a proverb that I absolutely love: "la charité bien ordonnée commence par soi-même" which means 'charity starts with caring for ourselves first' and this is not selfish, it's essential.

YASMINE IDRISS TANNIR (@PETITES_CHOSES)

I R I N I   T Z O R T Z O G L O U

OLIVE OIL, ALMOND, APRICOT & TAHINI CAKE

PREPARATION TIME: 20 MINUTES | COOKING TIME: APPROX. 1 HOUR 15 MINUTES | SERVES 8-10

In the Greek Orthodox Church we often fast from meat and dairy, but Greeks are infamous for their sweet tooth and we don't like going without cake! I tried many different variations of ingredients before settling on this delicious recipe.

INGREDIENTS

FOR THE CAKE

75g dried apricots
60ml brandy
225g self-raising flour
½ tsp baking powder
125ml extra-virgin olive oil
75ml sunflower oil
125g icing sugar
½ an orange, zested
½ a lemon, zested
75g ground almonds

FOR THE TOPPING

1 tbsp flaked almonds
1 tbsp sesame seeds
2 tbsp tahini
2-3 tbsp apricot jam

METHOD

Preheat the oven to 180°c. Grease a pretty cake tin then dust with flour.

Put the flaked almonds and sesame seeds for the topping in a dry frying pan and toast over a medium to high heat, shaking the pan from time to time to avoid them burning. Transfer to a small plate and set aside.

FOR THE CAKE

Finely slice three of the dried apricots and reserve them for the topping.

Roughly chop the rest and soak them in the brandy for 15 minutes.

Sift the flour with the baking powder into a bowl.

In another larger bowl, whisk the olive and sunflower oils with the sieved icing sugar for a few minutes. Add the orange and lemon zest, the soaked apricots and half the brandy. Mix with a spatula then gradually fold the flour and ground almonds in.

Use the remaining brandy to soak the sliced apricots for the topping.

Spoon the cake mixture into the prepared cake tin and bake in the preheated oven for 10 minutes, then reduce the heat to 160°c and continue baking for another 50 to 55 minutes.

Check that a thin knife or skewer comes out clean when inserted in the cake to test whether it's done, then leave to cool for 10 minutes and turn out onto a pretty plate.

FOR THE TOPPING

If the tahini is very thick, add a tablespoon of sunflower oil to loosen it then drizzle over the cake. In a small saucepan, heat the apricot jam with two tablespoons of water. Drain the sliced apricots and mix the brandy into the apricot jam.

Stir the jam and then drizzle it over the tahini on the cake. Finish by sprinkling the cake with the toasted flaked almonds, sesame seeds and sliced apricots.

Beyond caring about what we put in our bodies, we would serve ourselves well to stop the negative internal chat that tells us things like 'I could never be as good as this chef or that author or that cook'. We are all better than we think we are; we should see cooking as an opportunity to have fun and take great pleasure from creating something tasty and pretty. If something goes wrong in the process, it does not matter. Our inner self and others will enjoy it because of the love and good energy that went into its preparation!

IRINI TZORTZOGLOU (@IRINITZORTZOGLOU)

ESTHER CLARK

RASPBERRY, ROSE & PISTACHIO ETON MESS

PREPARATION TIME: 30 MINUTES | SERVES 4-6

Easy yet so fancy! You could switch this up by replacing the raspberries and pomegranate with caramel and banana, or classic strawberry with a glug of elderflower cordial.

INGREDIENTS

400g raspberries

1 tsp rosewater

400ml double cream

100g full-fat Greek yoghurt

2 tbsp icing sugar

1 tbsp pomegranate molasses

4 meringue nests, crushed

70g pomegranate seeds

50g pistachios, very finely chopped

Dried rose petals, to garnish

METHOD

Blitz half the raspberries in a food processor with the rosewater.

Strain through a sieve to remove the seeds.

In a large bowl, whisk together the double cream, yoghurt and icing sugar until you have a thick but spoonable mixture (try not to overbeat at this stage).

Gently fold the raspberry puree and pomegranate molasses through the cream mixture.

Spoon into four or six glasses, depending on their size, layering up with the crushed meringue and remaining raspberries.

Top each one with the pomegranate seeds, pistachios and rose petals.

I was quite an anxious child and discovered cooking was a great way to deal with that from a young age. To look after my mental health as an adult, I cook, write and occasionally do a little bit of painting! I also love music, so listening to some tunes while cooking is a great therapy for me. If I could give my younger self some advice it would be: breathe, don't overthink and above all don't worry about what others think of you.

ESTHER CLARK (@ESTHERMCLARK)

PEANUT BUTTER & CHOCOLATE BABKA

PREPARATION TIME: 35 MINUTES, PLUS 4 HOURS PROVING | COOKING TIME: 45 MINUTES | MAKES 2 LOAVES (SERVES 16)

Cooking has always brought me joy when life gets difficult. I love the idea of giving people recipes that could brighten their day, and this is one of my favourite things to eat so hopefully you will enjoy it too!

INGREDIENTS

FOR THE DOUGH

550g strong white flour

Pinch of salt

7g dried yeast

100g caster sugar

100ml whole milk

4 large eggs

150g unsalted butter, softened and diced

FOR THE FILLING

125g dark chocolate, finely chopped

100g smooth peanut butter

50g unsalted butter, diced

50g dark brown sugar

30g cocoa powder

Large pinch of flaked sea salt

TO FINISH

100g caster sugar

50ml water

50g salted peanuts, roughly chopped

METHOD

FOR THE DOUGH

Heat the milk until warm but not hot, then set aside. Put the flour in the bowl of a stand mixer that has a dough hook. Add the salt on one side and the yeast with the sugar on the other, as too much exposure to the salt will kill the yeast. Mix each side into the flour with your hands, then mix it all together with the dough hook.

Pour the warm milk into the flour with the mixer running until combined. With the dough hook on a medium speed, gradually add the eggs and mix for 10 minutes until you have a smooth dough. Gradually add the softened butter, one or two cubes at a time, until combined. This will take another 5 to 8 minutes. Scrape down the sides of the bowl. The dough will be very soft.

Transfer the dough into a large bowl, cover with a tea towel and leave for 1 and a half to 2 hours until doubled in size and well-risen.

Once risen, put the dough in the fridge for 1 hour.

FOR THE FILLING

While the dough is chilling, line the bottom and sides of two 23 by 10cm loaf tins with non-stick baking paper then make the filling. Put all the ingredients into a small saucepan over a low-medium heat, stirring to prevent anything from catching on the bottom until everything has melted together. Transfer the mixture to a bowl and cool for 30 minutes until almost set.

TO ASSEMBLE THE BABKA

Take the dough out of the fridge and split into two equal pieces. Lightly flour your work surface and roll the dough out into a 30 by 40cm rectangle. Spread half of the filling onto it, leaving a 1cm border around the edge. Starting from the shorter side, roll the dough up into a tight spiral, placing the join underneath. Using a sharp knife, halve the roll lengthways so you have two long pieces. Cross them over each other repeatedly until you have a braid-like pattern, then place the loaf into one of the prepared tins. Repeat this whole process with the other piece of dough. Cover and set aside to prove for 1 hour until doubled in size.

TO BAKE AND FINISH THE BABKA

Preheat the oven to 180°c and bake the loaves for 35 to 40 minutes until golden.

Heat the sugar and water together and simmer for 4 minutes to make a loose syrup. Once out of the oven, brush the babka with the syrup, sprinkle with the peanuts and leave to cool before slicing.

BUTTERMILK BANANA BREAD

PREPARATION TIME: 15 MINUTES | COOKING TIME: APPROX. 45 MINUTES | SERVES 4-6

The perfect breakfast treat, and a great way to use up open pantry boxes and bags. It's the ultimate midweek pick-me-up or something to take your weekend brunch to the next level.

INGREDIENTS

284ml buttermilk
120g oats
1 very ripe banana
1 tsp cinnamon
1 tsp vanilla extract
1 tsp bicarbonate of soda
Pinch of salt
2 eggs
100g nuts and seeds
100g dark chocolate chips

METHOD

Preheat your oven to 180°c fan.

Add the buttermilk and oats to a large bowl and mix thoroughly, then set aside while you prepare the other ingredients, giving the oats some time to absorb the buttermilk.

Peel and crush the banana, then combine it with the cinnamon, vanilla, bicarbonate of soda and salt. Next, mix the eggs into the oats and buttermilk until fully incorporated. Add the nut and seed mix, mix thoroughly, then stir in the banana mixture followed by the chocolate chips.

Give the batter one really good last mix. This is really important to make sure the bicarbonate of soda is evenly distributed, treating it like a soda bread (which is really what it is).

Place the mixture into a lined two litre loaf tin, and bake for 40 to 50 minutes in the preheated oven until golden brown and forming a light crust.

I totally shouldn't, but I love this banana bread straight out of the oven when the chocolate is melting everywhere! It's best just as it is, especially if you have no patience at all! I also love to bake a loaf for the week ahead; it's delicious for breakfast, toasted and brushed with a generous amount of honey.

If you are struggling to find buttermilk, don't stress! You can replace it with the same amount of Greek yoghurt or a good quality thick natural yoghurt. For the nut and seed mix, I use a combination of granola, sunflower seeds, pumpkin seeds, linseeds and desiccated coconut. Feel free to go wild though, this is the ultimate leftover recipe and you can add pretty much any dry ingredients from your pantry.

Mental health is so very important in the kitchen. Personally, I think I have spent my entire career telling people how great everything is and most of the time not being honest. Having the freedom to talk about how you feel is amazing and sometimes the most refreshing feeling. I let my career take over my entire life and that resulted in a lot of jealousy and upset from missing out on life events and time with my friends. Take time for yourself, think about your happiness and don't be afraid to reassess everything constantly.

OLIVIA BURT (@CHEFLIVBURT)

CARLA HENRIQUES

STICKY TOFFEE PUDDING

PREPARATION TIME: 15 MINUTES | COOKING TIME: 25 MINUTES | SERVES 10

We've had this on the menu at Hawksmoor since day one. The recipe was tweaked over a few years until we got the perfect balance. It's always been our best seller and is definitely one of the best in London.

INGREDIENTS

FOR THE TOFFEE SAUCE

250g unsalted butter

250ml double cream

125g dark muscovado sugar

125g light muscovado sugar

Generous pinch of sea salt

FOR THE TOFFEE PUDDING

250g dates, finely chopped

6g bicarbonate of soda

375ml boiling water

82g unsalted butter

125g dark muscovado sugar

125g light muscovado sugar

2 large eggs

338g self-raising flour

6g baking powder

Generous pinch of sea salt

METHOD

FOR THE TOFFEE SAUCE

Gently heat all the ingredients in a saucepan until the butter and sugar have melted, then turn up the heat. When the sauce starts to simmer it's ready to serve.

FOR THE TOFFEE PUDDING

Preheat the oven to 180°c. Grease ten small dariole moulds, or individual ramekins. Put the chopped dates into a bowl with the bicarbonate of soda and boiling water, then leave to soak until the liquid is very dark.

Meanwhile, beat together the butter and muscovado sugars. Mix in the eggs one by one, followed by the flour, baking powder and salt. Lastly, beat the date mixture into the batter.

Fill the moulds or ramekins three quarters full, then bake in the preheated oven for 25 minutes, or until risen and cooked through.

Test with a skewer to see whether it comes out clean. Unmould the puddings and serve them with the warm toffee sauce and a big spoonful of clotted cream on top.

The importance of awareness for mental health and suicide prevention is very close to my heart, especially in this industry as we have lost some friends. I love my job and I love being a chef, but a lot of people have been affected by the stress levels and long hours. To look after my mental health, I got into exercise and now do lots of boxing, as well as reading and getting away at the weekend every time I can.

CARLA HENRIQUES (@CARLA_HENRIQUESS)

DATE NIGHT COOKIES

PREPARATION TIME: 45 MINUTES | COOKING TIME: 15 MINUTES | MAKES 12

If there was ever a dessert that perfectly described me, it would be this. It's full of chocolate, heart, and it comes from the Middle East. It's the best cookie to have around when you want something gooey and chewy!

INGREDIENTS

216g flour
40g cocoa powder
10g cornstarch
5g bicarbonate of soda
5g salt
150g butter, softened
140g light brown sugar
80g granulated sugar
10ml vanilla extract
1 egg
90g semi-sweet chocolate chips (around 60% cocoa content)
80g dates, chopped
25g pecans, chopped

METHOD

In a large bowl, sieve together the flour, cocoa powder, cornstarch, bicarbonate of soda and salt.

In another bowl with a wooden spoon, or a stand mixer fitted with a paddle attachment, beat the softened butter, brown sugar, granulated sugar and vanilla together until creamy. This should take about 5 minutes.

Add your egg and mix until incorporated, then gradually add your flour mixture and mix until just combined. Try not to overmix the dough because that makes the cookies tough. Fold in your chocolate chips, dates and pecans.

Scoop the dough into about 12 heaped tablespoons, shape them into balls and place on a baking tray lined with baking parchment. Make sure to space them out because they'll spread quite a bit.

Chill the cookie dough in the fridge for at least 30 minutes.

Bake the chilled cookies at 180°c fan for 13 minutes.

Take them out of the oven, let them cool (if you can wait) and then enjoy!

This issue means a lot to many people that don't often get the help they need. If we can help even one person out with this book, that would be amazing! Cooking helps me to look after my mental health because it's a meditative practice for me. I bake and go to another world because I'm at peace and so content with where I am. Spending time with my husband and dog, talking to my family, and walking a lot help too. I would also say listen to your thoughts. They're trying to tell you something!

HAYA KHALIFEH (@BUTTERBELIEVEIT)

SAFIA SHAKARCHI

RICOTTA, HONEY & SESAME ICE CREAM

PREPARATION TIME: 15 MINUTES, PLUS AT LEAST 8 HOURS FREEZING | MAKES ABOUT 8 SCOOPS

A lot of my cooking stems from my heritage, and it was actually food that brought me closer to my roots as a second generation Arab immigrant. I realised that I loved those flavours, and they just felt like home.

INGREDIENTS

250g ricotta
120g honey
100g tahini
300ml double cream
Sea salt

TO SERVE

Sesame seeds
Honey
Fresh figs (optional)

METHOD

Combine the ricotta, honey and tahini with a splash of the double cream and a generous pinch of sea salt in a medium-size mixing bowl. Whisk until smooth then set aside.

In the bowl of a stand mixer or using an electric whisk, whip the remaining double cream just to soft peaks.

Carefully fold the ricotta mixture into the whipped cream with a spatula.

Make sure it's well combined, but it's fine to still have some swirls of tahini and honey in there too.

Pour the mixture into a 900g (2lb) loaf tin or other freezable container, cover with cling film and pop in the freezer for at least 8 hours or ideally overnight.

Remove the ice cream from the freezer a couple of minutes before you want to serve, to allow it to soften.

Scoop into bowls and sprinkle with sesame seeds. You can add an extra drizzle of honey and some fresh figs too, if you like.

When I was living abroad and struggled settling into a new city, I turned to food for comfort. I photographed all the restaurants and cafes I went to and I started a food blog as a kind of 'diary'. I found a lot of solace in that. I was at university and had planned on working in an entirely different field, but I knew food was what I really loved so I took a risk and decided to try and make a career out of it. I think that's the biggest and best decision I've ever made. I am so incredibly glad I did.

SAFIA SHAKARCHI (@DEARSAFIA)

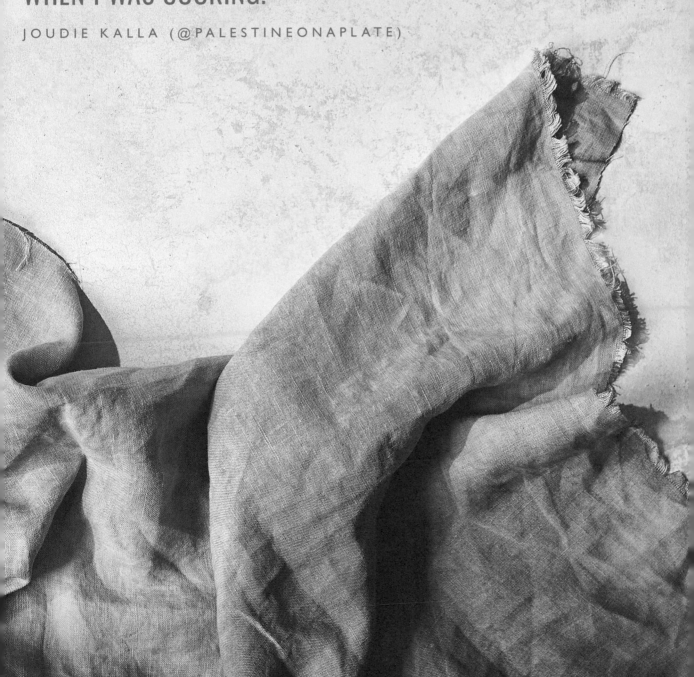

COOKING HAS BEEN A HUGE PART OF MY LIFE
AND MY MENTAL HEALTH WAS A HUGE PUSH
TO TURN THIS INTO A CAREER.

I FOUND PEACE IN THE KITCHEN AND IT QUIETENED
MY MIND, HELPING ME PUT MY DEPRESSION AT BAY
WHEN I WAS COOKING.

JOUDIE KALLA (@PALESTINEONAPLATE)

SEASONAL FRUIT CRUMBLE

PREPARATION TIME: 10 MINUTES | COOKING TIME: 20-30 MINUTES | SERVES 6-8

Finishing your day with something warming and nourishing can bring pleasure and comfort, and that's why I'm sharing this crumble recipe. Spending half an hour or so putting this together is a gentle act of kindness towards yourself or others.

INGREDIENTS

FOR THE TOPPING

140g light muscovado sugar

120g spelt flour

100g jumbo oats

50g desiccated coconut

50g pumpkin seeds

50g buckwheat groats

40g flaked almonds

40g hazelnuts, blanched and skins removed

½ tsp ground cardamom

Pinch of salt

150g butter, melted

FOR THE FILLING

700g mixed seasonal fruit (such as peaches, raspberries, cherries, plums, pears, blackberries, apples and rhubarb)

50g golden caster sugar

Knob of butter

METHOD

FOR THE TOPPING

Combine all of the dry ingredients in a bowl and then pour over the melted butter. Mix thoroughly with a spoon until a crumble consistency forms. If you want to cook it separately to keep in a jar and use as a quick topping for poached fruits, yoghurt or ice cream, preheat the oven to 180°c fan.

Spread the crumble mixture out in an even layer on a baking sheet and bake for 30 minutes. Alternatively, keep the raw crumble mixture in a tupperware in the fridge until you plan on using it; it will keep for a few days.

FOR THE FILLING

Prepare your chosen fruit; core and chop apples and pears, de-stone peaches, cherries and plums. Grease a pie dish with butter and fill it with your prepared fruit. Toss in the sugar and butter and mix everything well. Spoon over a tablespoon of water and cover with the crumble topping.

Bake at 180°c fan for 20 to 30 minutes, until the topping is crisp and golden and the filling is bubbling up the sides. Serve with cream or ice cream, always.

This topping is comforting and buttery, as every crumble should be, but it's also nourishing and packed full of goodness in the form of oats, nuts and seeds.

This is not your average crumble topping; it's full of texture and is almost like a cross between a granola and a crumble. In fact, it works really well as a lovely topping for yoghurt and fruit in the morning.

The fantastic thing about this is that you can vary the ingredients throughout the year, according to what you've got in and what's in season and at its best. You can also get ahead by making the crumble topping and keeping it in the fridge, or bake it and use it as and when.

My mental health has suffered throughout my life at the hands of stress, anxiety, grief and hormones. But I've been incredibly lucky that my problems have been relatively low key compared to some of my loved ones. I've always felt that one of the things I can do to help, other than listening and being there to support them, is to make delicious, wholesome food for them to eat. So often when we're feeling low, this goes out the window as the impetus to look after yourself gets lost, but there couldn't be a more crucial time to eat well.

ROSIE BIRKETT (@ROSIEFOODIE)

ROASTED STRAWBERRY KEFIR ICE CREAM

PREPARATION TIME: 15 MINUTES, PLUS 8 HOURS FREEZING | COOKING TIME: 1 HOUR | SERVES 6-8

This ice cream doesn't require churning, so it's easy to make without a machine. Kefir is a fermented milk drink similar to a thin yoghurt, and its slight tang goes really well with the intense flavour of the roasted strawberries.

INGREDIENTS

1kg British strawberries, washed, hulled and halved

Generous drizzle of honey

Sea salt

300ml double cream

200ml kefir

1 x 397g tin of condensed milk

Basil leaves, to garnish

METHOD

Preheat the oven to 120°c. Arrange the prepared strawberries on a large roasting tray lined with baking parchment. Drizzle them with honey and a pinch of salt. Pop in the preheated oven and roast for around 1 hour until caramelised.

Reserve a small bowl of the roasted strawberries in their cooking syrup for the garnish. Blitz half of the remaining strawberries in a food processor and set to one side.

In a large bowl, whip up the double cream with the kefir until it starts to form stiff peaks and thicken.

Beat in the condensed milk then fold through the intact roasted strawberries.

Scoop the mixture into a freezable container and stir through the roasted strawberry pulp to create a marbled effect. Freeze for at least 8 hours.

Serve each person a few scoops of ice cream with some reserved roasted strawberries on top (they should be sticky and cold by now), a drizzle of the syrup and a few small basil leaves.

TIRAMISÙ AL CIOCCOLATO

PREPARATION TIME: 3 HOURS | COOKING TIME: 30 MINUTES | SERVES 4

This dessert is my take on the classic tiramisu. It's a fairly new creation but has been a success since I showcased it on BBC MasterChef: The Professionals. For the more adventurous, I suggest adding some hazelnuts for extra texture.

INGREDIENTS

FOR THE COCOA CRUMBLE

125g flour

80g unsalted butter, diced and at room temperature

40g caster sugar

25g cocoa powder

FOR THE COFFEE JELLY

100ml espresso

20g sugar

5g edible gelatine leaf

25ml coffee liqueur

FOR THE MASCARPONE MOUSSE

4 egg yolks

100g sugar

6g edible gelatine leaf

100ml sweet wine (passito or moscato)

250g mascarpone

50g whipping cream

FOR THE CHOCOLATE GANACHE

80g egg yolk

35g sugar

150ml double cream

100ml milk

150g dark chocolate (55%)

4g edible gelatine leaf

METHOD

FOR THE COCOA CRUMBLE

Knead all the ingredients together to make a smooth dough. Wrap in cling film and leave to rest in the fridge for around 30 minutes. Preheat the oven to 180°c. Roll the dough out to form a 2cm thick sheet. Bake in the oven for 12 minutes. Let it cool, then break up to a crumble consistency. Set some aside and use the rest as a base for the tiramisu in your moulds or dish.

FOR THE COFFEE JELLY

Boil the coffee with the sugar. Soak the gelatine in cold water. Once the coffee is hot and the sugar has melted, remove from the heat. Squeeze the gelatine to remove any excess water. Drop into the coffee and whisk. When the mixture has cooled down, add the coffee liqueur.

FOR THE MASCARPONE MOUSSE

Whisk the egg yolks with the sugar until the mixture becomes pale white. Meanwhile, soak the gelatine in cold water. Separately, bring the sweet wine to boiling point. When the wine is hot, squeeze out the gelatine and allow it to melt in the wine. Pour the hot wine into the egg mixture then let it cool. Fold the mascarpone into the egg mixture. In a different bowl, whip the cream. Fold the cream into the mascarpone mixture to create a light and soft mousse.

FOR THE CHOCOLATE GANACHE

This is the centrepiece of the dessert. Beat the egg yolk with sugar. In a saucepan, bring the cream and milk to boiling point. Pour the hot mixture into the egg yolk and sugar. Whisk thoroughly and put the mixture back onto the heat. Meanwhile, break the chocolate into pieces and soak the gelatine leaf. Let the mixture reach 80°c then pour it onto the chocolate. Mix until melted and smooth. Squeeze out the soaked gelatine and add it to the hot chocolate ganache.

Once the chocolate ganache cools down, but is still liquid, pour it over the crumble (leaving space for the coffee jelly layer) then chill in the fridge for a couple of hours. Once the ganache has set, gently reheat the coffee jelly and drop a spoonful of it on top of the ganache. Return to the fridge for a minimum of 15 minutes.

TO SERVE

Put the tiramisu on the plate and pipe the mascarpone mousse on top. Dust with cocoa powder and serve with chocolate, hazelnut or coffee ice cream on the side.

HONEY CAKE WITH LEMON & CORIANDER SEEDS

PREPARATION TIME: 20-25 MINUTES | COOKING TIME: 50 MINUTES | SERVES 8-10

I would put coriander seeds in everything if I could get away with it! In my mind they are good wherever you would think to add lemon, so here one of my favourite cakes has had a reinvention using both.

INGREDIENTS

200g unsalted butter, at room temperature

200g golden caster sugar

4 medium-size organic eggs

150g white spelt flour

2 unwaxed lemons, zested and juiced

6 tbsp runny honey

1 tbsp coriander seeds, toasted and crushed to a fine powder

1½ tsp baking powder

150g ground almonds

FOR THE SYRUP (OPTIONAL)

½ a lemon, juiced

½ tbsp honey

1 tbsp coriander seeds

METHOD

Preheat your oven to 190°c or 170°c fan.

Grease a 24cm cake tin with a little butter, then line it with greaseproof paper.

First, beat the butter and sugar together in a large mixing bowl until light and fluffy.

You can do this in a stand mixer or with a handheld whisk if you like.

Crack in one egg, add a tablespoon of flour and beat until mixed in, then do the same with the other three eggs. Stir in the lemon zest, lemon juice and honey.

In a separate bowl, mix the ground coriander seeds, remaining flour, baking powder and ground almonds together with a whisk until there are no lumps.

Mix the dry ingredients into the honey mixture until everything is combined.

Spoon the mixture into the lined tin and smooth out the top.

Bake in the preheated oven for 50 minutes, until golden brown on top. The honey will make it brown quicker than a normal sponge cake, so if needed cover the tin with foil to stop the top browning any further.

When the cake is done, remove it from the oven and leave to cool in the tin before turning out and slicing.

If you want to add the syrup, gently heat the lemon juice, honey and coriander seeds together in a small pan then pour or spoon over the cake while both the cake and syrup are still warm. It's sweet, heady and not at all savoury.

*Recipe from The Modern Cook's Year by Anna Jones, published by 4th Estate.

Our mental health should be given as much care and attention as our physical health. I have struggled with this at times but through the support of family, friends and doctors I have always found my way back to my centre. Everyone should have access to that support. Also, there are few things that a cup of tea and a piece of cake will not help. This might sound trite but I believe it to be true.

ANNA JONES (@WE_ARE_FOOD)

SALTED CARAMEL TART

PREPARATION TIME: 50 MINUTES, PLUS CHILLING OVERNIGHT | COOKING TIME: UP TO 1 HOUR 30 MINUTES | SERVES 12

This has become a staple throughout my career; it was one of the first things on the menu when I started my bakery, Lockdown Loaves, and is possibly one of my all-time favourite desserts!

INGREDIENTS

FOR THE SWEET PASTRY

200g caster sugar

300g butter

2 eggs, beaten

500g flour

4g salt

FOR THE SALTED CARAMEL

500g double cream

140g caster sugar

135g egg yolks

35g muscovado sugar

Salt, to taste

METHOD

FOR THE SWEET PASTRY

Beat the sugar and butter together in a stand mixer, slowly pour in the eggs, then gradually add the flour and salt in three parts.

Work everything together until the mixture forms a soft dough, then cover and chill your pastry in the fridge overnight.

Roll out the chilled pastry, line your tart tin with it, trimming off any overhang, then rest in the fridge for 30 minutes. Blind bake the tart case at 180°c for around 30 minutes, checking now and then to make sure it's on the right track.

The pastry should be golden and firm when done.

I would recommend using a 28cm (11 inch) tart tin here, but you could easily adapt the recipe to fit different sized tins.

FOR THE SALTED CARAMEL

Wam the double cream over a gentle heat.

Meanwhile, melt your caster sugar in a separate pan and have the yolks and muscovado sugar mixed together in a separate bowl ready to use.

When the sugar in the pan has turned into a golden caramel, very gradually add the warm cream while mixing gently. Be very careful not to burn yourself as it will bubble up and emit a lot of very hot steam.

Once the cream and caramel are combined, gradually pour in the egg and sugar mixture while stirring continuously. Add salt to taste and then pass the mixture through a fine sieve to remove any lumps.

Pour the salted caramel filling into the pre-baked tart case and bake at 100°c until the centre of the tart is no longer liquid, but still has a slight wobble.

Check after 30 minutes and keep an eye on it; the total baking time could be up to an hour depending on your oven.

When done, leave the tart to cool at room temperature before slicing and serving.

I think that, especially during the recent pandemic, mental health has become the forefront of everyone's lives and it has become even more important to try our best to tackle it. My advice would be: always be true to your own feelings; they are the most important thing to protect. I like to get out to the sea to clear my head, and I think cooking acts as a form of therapy for me; it definitely balances out my mind.

HANNAH CATLEY (@HANNAHCATLEY)

FLOURLESS CHOCOLATE CAKE

PREPARATION TIME: 20 MINUTES | COOKING TIME: APPROX. 20 MINUTES | SERVES 8-10

This is a recipe I developed during lockdown, something really delicious that people could bake from scratch and be proud of. It's traditionally quite a hard cake to master but this recipe makes it really achievable.

INGREDIENTS

90g dark brown sugar

35g cocoa powder

1 tsp baking powder

125g unsalted butter

225g dark chocolate

4 eggs

Handful of pecans (or walnuts or hazelnuts)

Pinch of sea salt (optional)

METHOD

You will need an 18cm cake tin (a 20cm or 23cm one would do) as well as a whisk, two bowls, a saucepan and some baking paper.

Preheat your oven to 180°c. Use some butter to grease the cake tin and stick the baking paper in place, lining the base and sides. The paper should be too big for the tin and stick out above the edges.

Whisk your sugar, cocoa powder and baking powder together evenly then set aside. Chop the butter and chocolate into small pieces then melt them together in a bain-marie (a metal or glass bowl placed over a saucepan with a few centimetres of water in it) over a medium heat.

Stir until they have slowly melted, combined and cooled. My top tip is to take the bowl off the heat three quarters of the way through melting. Your mixture will cool as the rest of the chocolate melts. Alternatively, you can put the butter and chocolate in a microwave-proof bowl and melt for 1 minute 30 seconds in 30 second intervals, stirring after each blast.

In another bowl, beat your eggs well with a whisk for around 20 seconds by hand. Add the egg to the cooled chocolate mixture, and beat it all together with the whisk, again by hand, until it starts to look glossy.

Add the whisked sugar, cocoa and baking powder to the bowl and stir to combine the mixtures evenly. Tip the cake batter into the prepared tin so it sits level.

Scatter your choice of nuts on top, followed by some Maldon or other sea salt. This is optional but highly recommended! Bake in the preheated oven for 19 to 20 minutes for an 18cm tin. If you're using a bigger tin, check it after 18 minutes.

Your cake should be just set on top but wobbly when you gently shake the pan, because you want a lovely gooey centre. It's normal for the cake to rise and then sink once it's cooled. It will keep well for 4 to 5 days.

Mental health is such an important issue, one that affects everyone to varying degrees and too often goes unchecked. It's important to look after each other and look out for those who might need our support. Baking is very calming and has been key for managing my own mental health in times of stress or grief. Something about the way you're very focused and engrossed in the physical clears the mind and tuning out like that can be a huge relief, as well as the joy that comes from making something delicious from scratch and sharing it with others.

LILY JONES (@LILY_VANILLI_CAKE)

CHURROS & CHOCOLATE

PREPARATION TIME: 20 MINUTES | COOKING TIME: 20-30 MINUTES | MAKES ABOUT 30

My dad would take me into Málaga very early in the morning to beat the traffic, the heat and the crowds in the market. We would always eat churros and sip coffee, listening to the shop shutters rolling open nearby.

INGREDIENTS

FOR THE CHURROS

200g strong white bread flour

½ tsp fine salt

¼ tsp bicarbonate of soda

260ml warm water (70°c)

400ml sunflower oil, for frying

FOR THE CHOCOLATE SAUCE

100g dark chocolate (60-70% cocoa solids)

90ml double cream

30ml milk

METHOD

FOR THE CHURROS

Sift the flour with the salt and bicarbonate of soda into a large bowl. Whisk in the warm water until there are no lumps.

The mixture will benefit from resting for 5 to 10 minutes here.

In a small saucepan (so the oil is deep enough) heat the sunflower oil to 180°c.

Spoon the now thickened churro mixture into a piping bag. If you want ridges, use a star nozzle. Twist the bag so it's sealed and gently squeeze the mixture into the heated oil in 5 to 7cm pieces. You can use a pair of scissors to snip the dough at the nozzle. Do this in small batches.

Using tongs, turn the churros over as they fry and then lift them out when golden brown. Drain them on kitchen paper.

At this point, you can eat them as they are, roll them in cinnamon sugar or dip them in chocolate sauce.

FOR THE CHOCOLATE SAUCE

Chop the chocolate and put it in a heatproof bowl.

Bring the milk and cream to a simmer in a saucepan then pour the hot liquid over the chocolate.

It's important to let it sit for 1 minute before stirring into a smooth sauce ready for dipping.

Cooking has always been a form of escapism for me. Recreating a meal from a holiday can instantly transport me back to that time and place. Of course, if we are talking about happiness, then I love cooking for others. The Spanish have a tradition of 'sobremesa' which is the time spent after a meal relaxing and chatting. We do this in Spain even on a working lunch; how the Spanish eat is as important as what they are eating. Having friends over and taking your time at the table is one of life's greatest pleasures.

MILLI TAYLOR (@MILLITAYLOR)

LAURA TILT

DARK CHOCOLATE FRUIT & NUT BARK

PREPARATION TIME: 30 MINUTES | COOKING TIME: 5-10 MINUTES | SERVES 6 OR MORE

This is a delicious sweet snack which offers some heart-healthy fats and fibre. It's also incredibly fun to make!

INGREDIENTS

300g dark chocolate

1-2 tbsp peanut butter (optional)

75g mixed nuts and dried fruit (pistachios and cranberries are great for colour, almonds are great for crunch)

METHOD

Line a baking tray with baking paper.

Using a sharp knife, chop up the chocolate, place it into a bowl and gently melt over a pan of simmering water.

Take the bowl off the heat when about 70% of the chocolate has melted, then stir continuously until completely melted.

Pour the chocolate onto the prepared baking tray and carefully spread it out towards the edges with a palette knife. If you're using peanut butter, soften it slightly or stir until it is runny. Add blobs of peanut butter to the chocolate and use a knife to swirl them together.

Roughly chop the nuts then scatter the nuts and dried fruits evenly over the top of the chocolate.

Refrigerate the bark for about 15 minutes, until hardened.

Finally, invert the bark onto a chopping board, remove the parchment paper, break into pieces and store or serve.

Mental health is something we all have: it's a continuum. We're all on it, just at different places, and our position changes throughout our lives. Learning about our mental health, what helps to keep us balanced, and having people to talk to about how we feel is really important. Having struggled with depression twice in my life, I know that it takes incredible strength to get through the dark days, when it feels like the lights have been turned out. If you're struggling, please know you're not alone; help is available and you can recover and feel like you again.

LAURA TILT (@NUTRITILTY)

LEMON & CRANBERRY BAKED CHEESECAKE

PREPARATION TIME: 15 MINUTES | COOKING TIME: 40 MINUTES | SERVES 12

This cheesecake is a lighter option than traditional recipes, which can often be quite heavy and rich. Any dried fruit can be used here; I have used dried cranberries as they add a lovely colour to the filling.

INGREDIENTS

FOR THE BASE

50g unsalted butter

150g digestive biscuits

FOR THE FILLING

350g full-fat cream cheese (such as Philadelphia)

150g golden caster sugar

4 medium eggs

2 tsp vanilla essence

1 lemon, zested and juiced

1 handful of dried cranberries

300ml soured cream

METHOD

Preheat the oven to 180°c.

FOR THE BASE

Melt the butter in a small saucepan.

Break the digestive biscuits into chunks and place into a food processor. Whizz until you've got smooth crumbs. Transfer them to a mixing bowl and add the melted butter, stirring until all the crumbs are evenly coated.

Press the base mixture into the bottom of a lightly greased 20cm cake tin; this must be a tin with a removable collar. Press the mix firmly into the edges.

FOR THE FILLING

Place the cream cheese, caster sugar, eggs, vanilla, lemon zest and juice into a mixing bowl. Mix together until smooth and then stir in the cranberries.

Pour this mixture on top of the biscuit base then place the cheesecake in the preheated oven to bake for approximately 30 minutes until just set.

Remove from the oven at this point, as it continues to set while cooling.

After approximately 10 minutes, smooth the soured cream over the top of the cheesecake. Place it back into the oven and cook for a further 10 minutes.

Remove and allow the cheesecake to cool completely and set. Remove the collar of the cake tin and slide off the base onto a serving plate. Refrigerate until serving.

*From Tana Ramsay's Family Kitchen

RAW CHOCOLATE CHEESECAKE

PREPARATION TIME: 20 MINUTES, PLUS 2-3 HOURS SETTING | SERVES 8-10

Recipes like this have changed my relationship with chocolate and I have also transformed the attitudes of many others with my raw chocolate treats; they can be life changing!

INGREDIENTS

FOR THE BASE

140g almonds

40g oats

2 tbsp raw cacao powder

Pinch of salt

12 pitted Medjool dates (200g)

¼ tsp vanilla powder or essence

FOR THE FILLING

120ml coconut milk, chilled for about 4 hours

2 large ripe avocados

60ml maple syrup

20g raw cacao powder

½ tsp vanilla powder or essence

Pinch of salt

FOR THE CHOCOLATE SAUCE

2 tbsp raw cacao powder

2 tbsp melted coconut oil

Pinch of salt

METHOD

FOR THE BASE

Grease a 20cm loose-bottomed cake tin with a little bit of coconut oil.

If you are using a silicone mould of the same size, there's no need to grease it.

Put the almonds, oats, cacao powder and salt into a food processor. Blend until the nuts and oats have broken down. Add the dates and vanilla then blend again until the dates have broken down and you have a sticky mixture.

Transfer just over half of this mixture to your cake tin and press down firmly with the back of a spoon or your fingertips to create the base.

Spoon the remaining mixture around the edges of the tin and use your fingers to press upwards from the base, creating sides about 2.5cm in depth from the base.

Use a spoon to neaten the top of the crust.

FOR THE FILLING

Make sure your coconut milk has been in the fridge for about 4 hours so it solidifies. Halve and destone the avocados, scoop out the flesh and put it into the food processor with all the other ingredients.

Blend until completely smooth and creamy, then spoon the filling into the base.

FOR THE CHOCOLATE SAUCE

In a small bowl, mix the ingredients together until fully combined then drizzle the chocolate sauce on top of your cheesecake.

Finish by decorating it with chopped nuts, dried fruit, edible flowers, cacao nibs or anything else delicious, colourful and edible you can find in your cupboards!

Pop the decorated cheesecake into the freezer and leave it to set for about 2 hours, or 3 hours in the fridge, and it should be ready to eat. You can either keep this stored in the freezer for up to 3 months (it will need a little bit of defrosting before eating) or in the fridge for up to 5 days. If you used a silicone mould, you will need to completely freeze the cheesecake to remove it from the mould cleanly.

"
I always cook when I feel sad. I love the connection to food, and creating something delicious and healthy always lifts my soul. Meditation, yoga, journalling, walking in the woods, long baths, spending time with friends and reflecting are some of the other things I do to look after my mental health. If I could give my younger self some advice, it would be don't sweat the small stuff, and that you are enough and worthy of more than you know.

NAOMI BUFF (@NOURISHBYNAOMI)

I SURROUND MYSELF WITH PEOPLE
WHO MAKE ME FEEL GOOD.

ACCEPT WHERE I AM RIGHT NOW AND KNOW
THAT ANALYSING THE PAST OR WORRYING
ABOUT THE FUTURE IS FUTILE.

ALL WE HAVE IS NOW.

ANNA JONES (@WE_ARE_FOOD)

INDEX

Strawberries
   Strawberry Cinnamon Toast 32
   Strawberry Gazpacho 174
   Roasted Strawberry Kefir
   Ice Cream 198

Sumac
   Vegetarian Stuffed Peppers 70
   Red Lentil Hummus &
   Seasonal Vegetables 120

Sunflower seeds
   Coconut & Vanilla Granola 24
   Gluten-Free Superfood Bread 50
   Red Lentil Hummus &
   Seasonal Vegetables 120
   Buttermilk Banana Bread 186

Sweet potato
   Sweet Potato Fritters 40
   Roast Cauliflower with Coconut &
   Fermented Turmeric Mee Rebus 64

Szechuan pepper
   Lamb Shapta 152

T

Tahini
   Roasted Trout, Sesame Miso Dressing,
   Nori Puree & Yuzu Pickled Daikon 62
   Red Lentil Hummus &
   Seasonal Vegetables 120
   Tahini Chicken Schnitzel 138
   Butternut Squash Mac 'n' Cheese 172
   Olive Oil, Almond,
   Apricot & Tahini Cake 180
   Ricotta, Honey & Sesame
   Ice Cream 192

Tamarind
   Morning Elixir: Jamu Juice 20

Tarragon
   Flash Fried Courgettes
   with Green Sauce 122
   Bourbon BBQ Turkey
   Tarragon Burger 124
   King Prawn & Pea Risotto 150

Tempeh
   Plant-Based Buddha Bowl 54

Teriyaki sauce
   Plant-Based Buddha Bowl 54

Timur pepper
   Lamb Shapta 152

Tofu
   Plant-Based Buddha Bowl 54

Tortillas
   Mexican Beef & Jalapeño
   Quesadillas 86
   Harissa & Halloumi Quesadillas 100

Trout
   Roasted Trout, Sesame Miso Dressing,
   Nori Puree & Yuzu Pickled Daikon 62

Truffle oil
   Truffled Artichokes, Parmesan
   & Lemon 108

Turkey mince
   Bourbon BBQ Turkey
   Tarragon Burger 124

Turmeric
   Morning Elixir: Jamu Juice 20
   Roast Cauliflower with Coconut &
   Fermented Turmeric Mee Rebus 64
   Tarka Dal 74
   Turmeric Chai Protein Balls 80
   Tandoori Sea Bass &
   Bombay Potatoes 106
   Prawn Moilee 110
   Butternut Squash Mac 'n' Cheese 172

W

Walnuts
   Gluten-Free Superfood Bread 50
   California Walnut & Pomegranate
   Summer Salad 58
   Healthy Gut Wake-Up Shake 82
   Flourless Chocolate Cake 206

Watercress
   California Walnut & Pomegranate
   Summer Salad 58

White cabbage
   Fermented Asian Slaw 56

White miso
   Fermented Asian Slaw 56

White wine
   Roasted Trout, Sesame Miso Dressing,
   Nori Puree & Yuzu Pickled Daikon 62
   Broccoli Heart with
   Sabayon & Anchovy Crumb 68
   Spaghetti Vongole 116
   King Prawn & Pea Risotto 150

White wine vinegar
   Korean-Style Pork Tenderloin 136

Y

Yellow split peas
   Tarka Dal 74

Yoghurt
   Coconut & Vanilla Granola 24
   Smoothie Bowls 26
   Berry Kefir Overnight Oats 28
   Strawberry Cinnamon Toast 32
   Natural Yoghurt 76
   Yoghurt Pizza 88
   Raspberry, Rose & Pistachio
   Eton Mess 182
   Buttermilk Banana Bread 186
   Seasonal Fruit Crumble 196
   Roasted Strawberry Kefir
   Ice Cream 198

Yuzu juice
   Roasted Trout, Sesame Miso Dressing,
   Nori Puree & Yuzu Pickled Daikon 62

Z

Za'atar
   Baked Pomegranate Feta with Spiced
   Red Pepper Sauce & Tabbouleh 104

NOTES

This page is for your own notes about the recipes: ingredients you've swapped out, timings that work best for you and any additions that you or your family love... make them your own and have fun!

We hope you don't, but if you do come across any errors in the recipes, then you can let us know by emailing *inspire@beder.org.uk* and any updated recipes can be found at *www.beder.org.uk/frombederskitchen*